THE
COUNTRY GENTRY
IN THE
FOURTEENTH CENTURY

THE COUNTRY GENTRY
IN THE
FOURTEENTH CENTURY

WITH SPECIAL REFERENCE
TO THE HERALDIC
ROLLS OF ARMS

BY

N. DENHOLM-YOUNG

OXFORD
AT THE CLARENDON PRESS
1969

Oxford University Press, Ely House, London W.1

GLASGOW NEW YORK TORONTO MELBOURNE WELLINGTON
CAPE TOWN SALISBURY IBADAN NAIROBI LUSAKA ADDIS ABABA
BOMBAY CALCUTTA MADRAS KARACHI LAHORE DACCA
KUALA LUMPUR SINGAPORE HONG KONG TOKYO

© OXFORD UNIVERSITY PRESS 1969

PRINTED IN GREAT BRITAIN

INTRODUCTION

IN a general way this book may be regarded as a continuation of *Seignorial Administration in England* (1937) and *History and Heraldry* (1965). The outlook, in spite of the abundance of detail, is in the present volume somewhat broader than heretofore. The persons dealt with are for the most part the secular gentry of the fourteenth century, though the folk above and below them persistently intrude.

An interesting picture emerges in the following pages of Edward III's character and of his efficiency as an administrator and a commander-in-chief—until about 1360. On specific points, we seem to have here the first-known Clerk of the Council, Hugh de Kendal, preceding Gilbert de Roubiry. We find that the 'Monk of Malmesbury' was—and I do not know why I never thought of it before —probably a corrodar of Malmesbury Abbey. With the help of a slight knowledge of heraldry we have identified Thomas Turberville the Spy and Hugh his father. We have made suggestions about Lancaster King of Arms (Le Roi Bruiant?), the origins of Clarenceux, of Carlisle Herald, of Cotgrave's Ordinary, and—much more uncertain—of Cooke's Ordinary.

As for the Black Death, I am at a stand. The subject does not attract me, and therefore information and ideas alike elude my search. It is a relief to see that a much-needed study of the subject is forthcoming. I have therefore kept silent on this crucial topic, as also on the Peasants' Revolt, which might more suitably come into a later volume.

There may now be added to the Bibliography an able and interesting study written in French by Mr. L. J. Sutton of Robert de Ufford, an intimate friend of Edward I. It is published at Olne in Belgium (1968).

INTRODUCTION

The persons whom I would wish to thank for their kind help in the preparation of this work are numerous, but I must again single out Mr. Brynley Parry, the County Archivist of Caernarvon and an old friend also the Librarian and Mr. Alan Gyles-Jones of U.C.N.W., Bangor, and Miss Margaret Reaney. From the Printer and the Publisher I have received many kindnesses since I first approached Dr. Johnson about forty years ago. They continue to support me, in the French sense of the word, but not that only, with exemplary patience.

N. DENHOLM-YOUNG

at 10 *St. David's Road*
Caernarvon, N. Wales
Christmas Eve 1968

CONTENTS

ABBREVIATIONS	ix
ON THE SCOPE AND INTEREST OF THE ROLLS OF ARMS	xi
I. THE RANKS OF SOCIETY	1
II. THE KNIGHTS IN THE FOURTEENTH CENTURY	41
III. THE LOVETOT-LANGTON SCANDAL	73
IV. ROLLS OF ARMS OF EDWARD III'S REIGN (1327–1377)	89
V. PRIVATE ADMINISTRATION: THE HONOUR OF WALLINGFORD	121
VI. KNIGHTS IN TOURNAMENT AND AT WAR	132
APPENDIX I. The Caerlaverock and Galloway Rolls. The Stirling Roll	150
APPENDIX II. A Fourteenth-Century Knight-Errant: Sir Giles de Argentine	154
LIST OF WORKS CITED	156
INDEX	163

ABBREVIATIONS

Ann. Berm.	*Annales monasterii de Bermundeseia*, in *Annales Monastica*, vol. iii (R.S.)
Ann. Dunst.	*Annales prioratus de Dunstaplia*, in *Annales Monastica*, vol. iii (R.S.)
Ann. Lond.	*Annales Londonienses*, in *Chronicles of the Reigns of Edward I and II* (R.S.)
Ann. Mon.	*Annales Monastica*
Ann. Osen.	*Annales monasterii de Oseneia*, in *Ann. Mon.*, vol. iv (R.S.)
Ann. Paulin.	*Annales Paulini*, in Chronicles of the Reigns of Edward I and II, vol. i, 253–70
Ann. Theok.	*Annales monasterii de Theokesberia*, in *Ann. Mon.*, vol. i (R.S.)
Ann. Wigorn.	*Annales monasterii de Wigornia*, in *Ann. Mon.*, vol. ii (R.S.)
B.P.R.	*Black Prince's Register* (four vols. P.R.O. 1930–3)
C. Cl. R.	*Calendar of Close Rolls*
Cal. F.R.	*Calendar of Fine Rolls*
Cal. I.P.M.	*Calendar of Inquisitions Post Mortem*
I.P.M.s	*Inquisitions Post Mortem*
C.P.R.	*Calendar of Patent Rolls*
C.E.M.R.A.	A. Wagner, *A Catalogue of English Medieval Rolls of Arms* (Society of Antiquaries, 1950), published as vol. i of *Aspilogia, being Materials of Heraldry*
D.N.B.	*Dictionary of National Biography*
E.H.R.	*English Historical Review*
G.E.C.	G. E. Cokayne, *The Complete Peerage*, new edn. by V. Gibbs and others (1910 ff.)
Hem.	Walter Hemingburgh, *Chronicle*, ed. H. Rothwell for the Camden Society (1957)
L.Q.R.	*Law Quarterly Review*
Mur.	*Adae Murimuth Continuatio Chronicarum*, ed. E. M. Thompson (1889)
O.H.S.	Oxford Historical Society
Parl. Writs	F. Palgrave, *Parliamentary Writs and Writs of Military Summons, Edward I and Edward II*, Record Commission (1827–34)

ABBREVIATIONS

P.R.A.	Parliamentary Roll of Arms
P.R.O.	Public Record Office
Rot. Parl.	*Rotuli Parliamentorum*, six vols. (1783)
R.S.	Rolls Series
T.R.H.S.	*Transactions of the Royal Historical Society*
V.C.H.	*Victoria County History*
Y.A.J.	*Yorkshire Archaeological Journal*

ON THE SCOPE AND INTEREST OF THE ROLLS OF ARMS

Rolls of arms, in the heraldic sense, are nominal lists (sometimes in book form) of armigerous persons with the coats of arms to which they are or were entitled attached to their names. Only a handful of original parchment rolls remain for the reigns of Edward I and Edward II, and not a great many more for Edward III, but some hundreds of sixteenth- and seventeenth-century copies were made of these and of other lost originals by Robert Glover, Sir William Dugdale, and a score of less eminent antiquaries.

These documents vary in length from a few dozen names to more than a thousand, and in one or two late instances nearly two thousand. But in historical value they vary widely, for in the longer rolls persons who lived at widely different periods are included in a list that was added to from time to time, as leisure or opportunity allowed. Such rolls have sometimes grown by agglomeration. They were the work and property of heralds, to whom they represented an important capital asset or stock-in-trade. The rolls are divided for convenience into occasional, local, and general rolls. Occasional rolls are with one exception the most valuable, being nominal rolls of the earls, barons, and knights present at battles (Falkirk, Stirling, Bannockburn, Boroughbridge), sieges (Caerlaverock, Stirling, Calais), or tournaments (I and II Dunstable rolls). Local rolls are usually made for a county or group of counties, often based upon the great Parliamentary Roll of Arms, which assumed its present form early in the reign of Edward II (for which see my *History and Heraldry*) and is itself arranged by counties. General rolls, as their name forebodes, are inchoate, and like almost every medieval list of names bear no trace of alphabetical (or, indeed, any other) arrangement, except that it is customary to begin with a dozen or more potentates, living or long dead, fabulous or real, for these rolls were made by heralds for heraldic purposes, and the coats of arms are more important than those who bear them. If a coat, with the title, lies dormant, it may yet be revived in favour of a distant heir. The line may die out, but the coat could be modified and reassigned.

The herald led an anomalous existence. He was either a royal herald or a seignorial herald, i.e. in practice he could not (in our period) exist *in vacuo*: he needed a patron. Sir Henry Percy's king of arms was mentioned in the thirteenth century, and Henry Algernon Percy, Earl of Northumberland, still retained a herald and pursuivant in 1513.[1] Reasons have been given for assigning a number of thirteenth-century rolls to seignorial heralds,[2] and examples for the fourteenth century will be found in the following chapters.

These rolls reflect the changing structure and ideals of the society that gave them birth: the continued importance of the earls; the decrease of the purely legendary or fabulous entries, partly perhaps because the Arthurian cult had passed its zenith and Edward III's Knights of the Garter had their own Round Table, their own mystique; and, finally, the great extension of the armigerous class towards the end of the century by the inclusion of the squires. Before this, we have in the second quarter of the century a group of four rolls from the north of England that can be closely dated. Together they almost provide a list of knights of Edward III for that period.[3]

[1] Cited in Paul Murray Kendall, *The Yorkist Age*, 231, from *The Northumberland Household Book*, ed. Percy (1827).
[2] *History and Heraldry, passim.*   [3] Chap. IV *infra*.

I

THE RANKS OF SOCIETY

'When Adam delf and Eve span, who was then the gentleman?'

It seems to be accepted that we may speak of 'the country gentry' in the fourteenth century, and those of East Anglia are said to have helped to bring Edward III to the throne by supporting the invading party led by Queen Isabella and Roger Mortimer.[1] Yet John Ball, preaching to the rebel peasants at Blackheath in the course of the rising in 1381, is said to have asked (according to Walsingham) 'When Adam delf and Eve span, who was then the gentleman?'

We do not know whether, like 'Jesting Pilate' in regard to the broader issue 'What is truth?', he would not, according to Bacon, stay for an answer, but in writing of the fourteenth century we can hardly evade some attempt to pose and perhaps clarify this important sociological issue.

It was not only the 'belted knights' who became 'knights of the shire', but the class immediately beneath them. This is equally true of the whole administration of the country. The sheriffs, escheators, coroners, verderers, tax-collectors, and local justices were often not knights either: sometimes they were franklins—substantial free tenant farmers. There has been no general study of these people, knights and non-knights, who in the thirteenth century perhaps, and in the fourteenth century without dispute, may be labelled generically 'country gentry'. It has not fallen within the scope of

[1] M. McKisack, *The Fourteenth Century* (Oxford, 1959), Chap. I.

many who have written with some authority on the period[1] to tell us what they were like at home, to try and fill in the social background of this large, fluctuating, and indispensable body of men in the period of the three Edwards.

The amalgamation in war of knights and squires in the 1330s enormously enlarges the field to be worked by those who seek to use heraldry as an 'auxiliary science', though heraldically speaking the squires do not come into the picture, that is to say they are not found upon heraldic rolls until fifty years later. Most scholars could give some account of the Decline and Fall of the Sheriff, but important as it undoubtedly is in administrative history it is as nothing compared with the great social changes involved in the growth of the squirearchy, the country gentry of a later age.

A further complication of the subject is caused by the increasing secularization of the period. Though anti-papalism, anti-clericalism, and Lollardry do not concern us, the secularization of learning and literature alters the structure of government in all its aspects, central or local, royal or seignorial. Clerks and knights are found side by side with or in succession to one another in all manner of offices. The *miles literatus* is ceasing to be a rarity. Lewis de Beaumont's illiteracy (meaning he had no Latin) as exposed at his consecration was widely taken as a joke by contemporaries not because he was a knight banneret, but because he was a knight who could not read. Even in Edward III's reign most knights were expected to put up a better show than that.

Mr. Hunnisett, in a recent book on the medieval coroner, calls the officials who came from this class Buzones, as Bracton did. But Mr. Hunnisett appreciates

[1] An inquiry of this sort has played no part in the well-known works of Professors D. Pasquet, A. F. Pollard, and B. Wilkinson. They hardly ever mention a knight by name. Professor Gaillard Lapsley and Professor Cam blazed the trail in this direction, in articles that will be cited hereafter.

THE RANKS OF SOCIETY

that Bracton is applying the terminology of early-thirteenth-century plea-rolls to the situation as he saw it. It seems to me an excellent notion that, whatever the etymology of this word, Bracton had in mind simply the country gentry of the period, so that Mr. Hunnisett's book and my own are studies in the social, official, and warlike activities of the Buzones. Lapsley was excellent in his account of what they did, but his entymological excursions were tedious and, I think, misguided.[1]

The population of England in the Middle Ages is a moot point, but it is not vital to this inquiry, which is concerned only with certain classes of people who can be counted more easily. As to the total, the work of Professor Russell offers a useful basis.[2] Professor Russell believes that it was less than 4,000,000 before the Black Death, and fell to not more than 2,500,000 in 1377 after the recurrent plagues of the mid century, gradually rising again to not more than 5,000,000 in 1700, and, on the figures available for 1698, this book is concerned with one in twenty of the population. More confidence can be placed in the totals for the numerically small upper classes than in those for their less fortunate fellows, because the figures for 1698 came from a man whose professional life led him to study such matters, and at the same time fitted him so to do. For the controversial Gregory King, demographer and Lancaster Herald, would naturally take a keen interest in the number of potential fee-payers, but he had no need to 'declare his interest' as M.P.s do, for he derived no profit from assessing the size of the market for the exercise of his professional skills. And it was the business of heralds to estimate the number of persons present on any occasion,[3] and if necessary to prepare a roll of arms of them. It is

[1] Gaillard Lapsley in *E.H.R.* (1947), 177–93, 545–67.
[2] J. C. Russell, *British Medieval Population* (1948).
[3] Note that Nicholas Trivet reports from an heraldic source about the number of persons present at the Feast of the Swans in 1306. See my *History and Heraldry*, 13.

of some interest to find that King's conclusions for 1698 bear out those arrived at here by other methods for a period nearly four hundred years earlier.

The term 'country gentry' is a convenient one because it avoids the overtones of 'country gentlemen', of whom John Ball professed a judicial ignorance, for the ostensible purpose of advancing knowledge by finding an answer, but in fact to stimulate an incipient class feeling in the minds of his auditors. The heralds of course had their answer. A gentleman is a person of coat armour and a bastard is almost as bad as a mule, with no pride of ancestry or hope of posterity, but he can still have a coat of arms.[1] A wider view of gentry than that probably taken (though we have no explicit evidence for it at this date in England) by the knights themselves is explicitly adopted by the heralds and tacitly adopted by the king's ministers at Westminster and in the shire court. It was the remarkable rise of the squirearchy in the fourteenth century, a process that outlasted the Middle Ages, that prompted this view. The government was prepared, if necessary, to accept franklins or others as M.P.s, owing to a scarcity of knights, and the heralds by 1370 had accepted the squires as belonging to the armigerous class. The heralds in the mid-century took the view (like the continental view of *noblesse*) that if the father was a gentleman of coat armour all his sons up to the seventh were too. For these they were prepared to legislate, but after that the father could himself assign marks of cadency as differences for his eighth and further sons.[2] This remark has obviously wide implications. It opens wide the floodgates, but only in theory, for it had long been the practice for at any rate three or four sons of knights to be themselves armigerous. The problem was never serious in practice, because the rule of primogeniture forced the less well-

---

[1] Cf. the early treatise on heraldry in Bod. Lib. Ashm. roll 13A, which has some remarks on bastardy.

[2] Ashm. roll 15A. The little heraldic treatise is near the beginning of the roll.

endowed or landless younger sons to take holy orders, or become merchants or lawyers, the only other professions in which they could rise to fame and fortune unless they started humbly as lay clerks in the service of the king or of a magnate, lay or ecclesiastical. So in most families of country gentry the younger sons will be taught to read and write at the nearest school, and then sent to Oxford or Cambridge or put to the study of law in London, or apprenticed to a merchant. But the squires include, as well as younger sons, a larger class of tenants of fragmented fees, the victims or otherwise of subinfeudation, whose fathers had escaped knighthood, and who themselves did not aspire to be knights. These men are listed in the 1324 returns and are already styled *armigeri*, but as yet their arms are for use against the enemy and are not heraldic. Now none of the rolls examined for the period up to *c.* 1370 contain persons identifiable as not being knights; but in Sir Robert Laton's roll of *c.* 1370, as reported in the Scrope–Grosvenor controversy of *c.* 1385 in the Court of Chivalry, the esquires as a class are gentlemen of coat armour, and the word is ceasing to imply personal service to a lord or banneret. The table of Gregory King, whatever its value for present-day statisticians, is of prime importance to historians of other centuries before his own. It points the contrast, immediately obvious to the herald, in the position of the esquire at widely different dates and is a sure guide to the evolution of this class, and to its relation to the persons ranked above and below it.

In 1700 there were—though there had been remarkable fluctuations in the interval—as in the reign of Edward II, 160 temporal lords. The baronets (instituted by James I as an hereditary honour, which bannerets, now no longer created, were not) account for 1,400 families. There is no relationship between banneret and baronet, but by chance or not—possibly through the tenacity of feudal rights in land—the fluctuation is in names rather than numbers. There is a rise in status but the numbers decline somewhat. The 3,000 esquires would provide about two and a bit esquires for each knight.

It is below this rank that the shock really hits the medievalist. There are 12,000 families below the squires or gentlemen—just plain Mr. Smith, Gent., not Mr. Smith, Esq. So the esquire is now the squire, the lord of the manor, and the connotation has so changed that he is often enough a knight! Paradox can go no further. However, there was a drift both ways, and though some *valetti* became squires others became valets; honest knaves (*le valet* in the French pack of cards) became hardened criminals.

The main sociological problem that arises from John Ball's rhetorical question is therefore connected with the rise of the squires. In Henry III's reign and under Edward I, they went about like ribalds, beating each other with sticks, and they were not allowed to compete in tournaments. Restrictions were placed upon the number allowed to each knight, but in vain. In the fourteenth century the squires, owing to changing military tactics, are lumped together with the knights and sergeants as men-at-arms. This happens before the middle of the century. They are all *armigeri*, which becomes in the fifteenth century the common style of an esquire in legal documents. About 1370 the esquires had become armigerous in the heraldic sense, and are found upon the rolls of arms. The matter may be given perspective by a leap forward to 1698 for a brief look at the statistics of Gregory King.[1]

By this time the squires had climbed so high that 3,000 families of them are ranked above 12,000 families of gentlemen. Doubt has been cast upon King's figures, in various contexts, but chiefly, I suppose, by statisticians interested in the less fortunate classes of society which do

---

[1] Mr. King's table is conveniently reprinted in G. M. Trevelyan's *English Social History*, and he no doubt took it from his great-uncle Macaulay's celebrated first chapter, on 'the state of England in 1688'.

THE RANKS OF SOCIETY

not come within the scope of this inquiry. To the medievalist it is strange to rank squires above gentlemen. Whatever John Ball meant he did not mean this, but he and his fellows and the Wycliffites were disseminating an egalitarian philosophy of life—if his ranting may be so styled —that can very easily be taken out of context and used to support a modern doctrine of communism. Extremists in any age before or after this, through Levellers to Jacobins, have found help and comfort in such words, as others do in Kipling or *Mein Kampf*. But in 1381 this topsyturveydom had not yet arrived. The squires had only recently become heraldically armigerous, but they had thrown in their lot, as the franklins and yeoman farmers were to do, with the masters rather than with the men, and there was for a time an awkward gap between privileged and underprivileged persons.

There is no doubt about the nature of these social shifts, only about the numbers involved and their causes. If doubts are felt about King's figures for the classes here under consideration, it should be remembered that as a professional herald he had access to the evidence of the visitation records made by his colleagues or their predecessors in their progresses round their provinces to ascertain who had the right to bear arms, and to ensure that none bore arms to which he was not entitled. King needed this evidence in his capacity as a professional herald. It is possible that to modern economists these figures are of little importance: I have seen no comment. King, at any rate, would be interested enough to get his figures right, for as a professional he could have calculated—we do not know if he did so—from them in conjunction with the visitation records the number of potential clients. The chivalrous and potentially chivalrous classes together numbered, on his reckoning, 16,500 families. Since there were 5,000 lay knights' fees and so a class of 5,000 knights or potential knights at any period after the Conquest, if we allow two esquires to each knight, we shall not see a great difference in the number of families concerned as between 1300 and 1700, before the population explosion caused by the growth of towns and the Agricultural and Industrial Revolutions had altered the face of Merry England.

Clerks and Knights

The period of the three Edwards saw a number of promotions to the episcopate from the class of knights banneret who did much of the work of government in peace as well as in war. Louis de Beaumont was not the only knight to become a bishop. The civil service of the day was headed by wardrobe and, later, chamber clerks who ranked as bannerets in the royal household, and fought leading the king's knights as bannerets in the field. They were useful to the king in many capacities. Benstead, Droxford, and Moleyns may be taken as examples.

But these military clerks, until they were ordained bishops, were not what modern usage calls clerks in Holy orders but lay clerks, in minor orders, not priests who could claim benefit of clergy by reading 'the neck verse'.[1] It was the lay clerks, sometimes knights, who filled the ranks of a civil service swollen even in the fourteenth century, men trained at Oxford or in the study of law in London. The judicial bench as well as the episcopal throne could be approached via the tilt-yard. The Scropes are usually, and will here, too, be cited in evidence.

If clerk and knight do not always fuse in one person they are still more frequently to be found in the same family. A fluctuating group of magnates and a few thousand country gentry made up the ruling class.

The Fourteenth-Century Rolls of Arms

The later rolls of arms are unlike those described in my earlier book. They (except the dated rolls) lack any sense

---

[1] Ps. 1:1; *Beatus vir qui non abiit in via impiorum.*

of immediacy. Not only are they not (except Cooke's Ordinary) original or occasional, but they seem to be far removed from reality—from any immediate connection with the persons whose arms they purport to describe. We see through a glass darkly. A veil has been interposed between us and the court. There is an enormous gap between them and the P.R.A., which is authoritative, as all who have studied it have agreed. Not a word or line is wasted; it bears every mark of authenticity. It is not until the historian comes to deal (as a historian and without regard to their genealogical worth) with the rolls of Edward III's reign that he realizes the loss of reality. Even the best of them—Cooke and Cotgrave—are one step away from reality. These too are outstanding efforts, not very far from the court, having nothing to do with the field of battle, and so in no sense occasional, but originating in that sudden sense of glory that produced in and after Crécy a feeling of achievement that ought to be recorded. Though it produced no roll of arms, Crécy is commemorated in 'the great East window at Gloucester dateable on heraldic grounds between 1347 and 1349'.[1]

Heralds have always been onlookers, recording feats of arms in which they took no part. After the heroic age of Edward I they seem to lose touch with what is happening around them, though they were more than ever needed in the reigns of Edward II and Edward III, and their numbers multiplied. But the men who compiled the ordinaries are inevitably a few steps further away from the field of battle than the compilers of 'occasional' rolls.

Edward I had never been a prince before he conquered Wales in 1284. He then assumed the title and handed it down to his son in 1301. Before this he was *Dominus Edwardus*, and it is as well to remember that a monk— any monk—was equally *Dominus*: yet we do not speak of the Lord Matthew Paris. In the reign of Edward II the

[1] Joan Evans, *Medieval English Art* (1949), 53 and references. The window was given by Lord Bradston, who commanded a fifth part of the king's division.

difficulty becomes acute and Sir Robert Clifford of 1300 becomes Lord Robert Clifford, anticipating the cleavage between Lords and Commons of 1332. The difficulty was not felt in Latin or French. Edward's eldest son was 'Sire Aufonse', and 'Monsieur W. de Hever' and 'Monsieur de Valoynes' are not lords or even bannerets, but simple knights.

Much of what is written in this book could be brought under the title *The English Government at Work*, a title used in a composite and uneven volume, redeemed by a brilliant chapter on Parliament, the best since Maitland gave an impetus to the study of the subject in his edition of the petitions of 1305.[1] The intention here has been to add the social background, already sketched by Stubbs, and this is made easier by the use of the heraldic rolls of arms for the whole period.[2]

The subject is much wider in the fourteenth than in the thirteenth century, because of the rise of the squires. The *armigeri* are becoming armigerous in the heraldic sense. I have also extended the scope of my inquiry, somewhat arbitrarily, to glance at some of the younger sons of the nobility and gentry. They too were country gentry, if at all successful in life, and many made their way by taking Holy orders. To complicate the matter, there are a number of important examples of king's clerks in minor orders who ranked as knights banneret (e.g. Droxford, Benstede), and when ripe for promotion became bishops. Droxford is the best example of this kind of career. This is probably why, although a banneret, he is not in the P.R.A. He has become a bishop, being elected in February 1309.[3] Edward II tried in vain in 1323 to have him trans-

[1] F. W. Maitland, *Memoranda de Parliamento* (R.S. 1893).

[2] The remarkable fact that there are four overlapping rolls for the period 1334–5 has prompted me to make a combined index or *catalogue raisonée* of them as a companion to this volume.

[3] Though Droxford ranked as a banneret in the royal household—he and Benstede are at the end of the Falkirk roll of arms of 1298—he persecuted the tournament men unmercifully in the early years of the century. Perhaps his

THE RANKS OF SOCIETY

lated to some see outside the kingdom. It may be supposed that Edward I's war minister knew too much for the safety of some people. He had to have, as had all important clerks, a few rectories for his support—Droxford in Hampshire, Hemingburgh and Stillingfleet in Yorkshire, and as bishop a choice of sixteen manor houses on the episcopal estates. These were of course as essential as judges' lodgings to a judge on circuit for the proper performance of his duties.[1]

The parallel is not inapt for the fourteenth century, because retired or promoted king's clerks, if they did not become bishops, could become judges, as John Benstede (d. 1324?)[2] and later the Scropes. Perhaps this is why heraldry spread to the episcopate and judiciary: from the time of Peter des Roches, the able Poitevin Bishop of Winchester, knights could and did exchange the surcoat for the surplice, or, like the Bishops of Durham, would have a few of each at hand. It should be emphasized that most of the king's clerks who were styled knights were only in minor orders, not yet ordained priests. They were lay clerks, like choristers and organists, and so could sing or fight as they have so often done. 'Parsons' or 'lay rectors' are less of an anomaly.[3]

There is a pre-renaissance period in the fourteenth century when rich men collected manuscripts. Even if they

son John de Drakensford inherited this attitude, for in 1334–5 he refused to assume knighthood (*C. Cl. R.* 211). The father, Keeper of the Wardrobe for years, first appears as a king's banneret in Flanders in 1294 with 3 knights and 29 esquires. As Bishop of Bath and Wells (1309–29) he was pursued by demands for his accounts for eighteen years, until in 1327 it was decided to leave him in peace (*C. Cl. R.* 31). Droxford's arms at Falkirk were *quarterly or and azure with roses countercharged* (? one in each quarter).

[1] Bishop Hobhouse, *The Calendar of the Register of John de Droxford, Bishop of Bath and Wells, 1309–1329* (Somerset Record Society, 1887), is a most irritating but quite useful work. The administration of the diocese has, to me, no striking features. Private chantries and oratories are becoming popular (pp. 148, 163, 230).

[2] See *D.N.B.*

[3] The *persona* does not become the 'parson' in the modern colloquial sense until long after the period covered by this book.

do not read them, they can always look at the pictures. Three outstanding names occur in this category: though they are hardly country gentry in any sense of the term, they represent a trend that will later (but hardly, owing to the cost before the invention of printing) infiltrate the ranks of the country gentry. They might be able to read or even collect a library when it became fashionable to have one, but even then the majority can have had little use for books, except as patrons, for that came to be expected of a gentleman. Eventually the aristocracy, or the rich classes, had to replace the monks as patrons of learning. A start was made in the fourteenth century by Guy Beauchamp, Earl of Warwick (d. 1315), who in 1305 gave twenty-seven books to the Cistercian abbey of Bordesley in Worcestershire.[1]

The Bohuns, Earls of Hereford, too were patrons of literature. And, indeed, it is remarkable that tournaments, heraldry, and illuminated manuscripts go hand in hand in these two instances, as in others. The greatest collector of them all has been dealt with elsewhere—Richard de Bury, Bishop of Durham, and author of the Philobiblon.

It was possibly the increase of literacy which so helped forward the anti-clerical movement. Agitation against 'foreign clerks', foreign merchants, alien priories, and Templars gradually consolidated and merged with national, and, in part, anti-clerical, feeling—not only anti-papal feeling. Hence the first lay Chancellor Robert Bourchier is found in 1360, and at the same time a feeling becomes evident that Englishmen, and lay Englishmen at that, should manage their own affairs.

Anglicization

The spreading use of the English language in the fourteenth century was a big factor in the growth of

---

[1] N. Ker, *Medieval Libraries of Great Britain*, 2nd edn. (1964), 11.

THE RANKS OF SOCIETY

nationalism and anti-papalism. The manorial, hundred, and shire courts inevitably conducted their proceedings in the language of their suitors. Thus the use of English spread upwards from below: the lords spoke Anglo-Norman, but their tenants spoke English, and in 1362 English was officially adopted as the language of all royal courts of law. Next year the Chancellor opened Parliament in English. Sir John Mandeville wrote his travels in English about 1377. Wycliffe translated the Bible in 1382. The first extant English will is dated 1387. Lancaster claimed the throne in English in 1399. The language was much used in sermons and devotional literature. All this is well known. In another way parallel conclusions may be reached from the evidence of charters.[1] The anglicization of Anglo-Norman personal names is very marked in the twenties and thirties of the fourteenth century, e.g. De Aula becomes atte Hall and so Athall or even Hall. De Bosco or Dubois or Atte Wood, Atwood, or Wood.[2] Alternatively many Latin names drop the 'de' in or around the decade 1360–70.

National feeling like the use of the English language spread rapidly with the yeoman (franklin) archers and their longbows. A self-conscious nationalism was forced upon them by events, for their victories were known and the tangible results in the form of the spoils that they brought home with them were seen in every village inn and alehouse. By what the soldiers experienced in France those who stayed at home were, with the added horrors and economic effects of the Plague, made conscious of the value of their services. The prospects of 'getting even with their betters' was made terrifyingly easy for them.

---

[1] These conclusions were first reached in making a *Cartulary of the Archives of Christ Church, Oxford* (O.H.S., 1931). They were confirmed on calendaring another 10,000 or so medieval deeds from the archives of the Queen's College and St. John's College.

[2] Of two London citizens in 1325, perhaps father and son, one is called Reginald de Conductu, the other Reginald atte Conduyt the younger. *C. Cl. R.* (1323–7), 145, 337, etc.

Attempts to freeze wages and enforce villein services produced an energetic reaction when these various stresses combined under the influence of anti-clericalism. The archers who had won Crécy, Poitiers, and Najera did not themselves influence the Peasants' Revolt of 1381, but they had aroused the envy of their neighbours. Higden, the monk and chronicler of Chester, expresses one aspect of this growth of medieval jingoism in a well-known passage. Higden says of the English 'that people are curious that they may know and tell the wonders they have seen; they cultivate other regions, and succeed still better in distant countries than in their own . . . wherefore it is that they are spread so wide through the earth, considering every other land that they inherit as their own country. They are a race able for every industry.' Other popular notions had already prepared the way for Napoleon's notion of small shopkeepers by describing the English as perfidious and *caudatus* (or tailed).[1]

Much of this efflorescence of national feeling was embodied in the person and policies of Edward III, his merchants, his generals, and his archers. But he could not have moved a step without the solid backing of the country gentry, who continued to administer the country in peace and war.

The Country Gentry

The question posed by John Ball at the time of the Great Revolt in 1381 is the justification of much that follows. It seems to indicate a social awareness that is not often found in the Middle Ages, a consciousness of the processes of history that is quite unmedieval. Most of the art and literature of the period shows that men did not realize they were living in the Middle Ages, or taking part in the Hundred Years War. But in setting bounds to

[1] *Polychronicon Ranulphi Higden*, ed. C. Babington. (R.S. 1869), ii. 66, 68. See further John Taylor, *The Universal Chronicle of Ranulf Higden* (Clarendon Press, 1966).

THE RANKS OF SOCIETY

this inquiry the problem is inescapable: who were the country gentry? Chronologically the period between 1310 and 1377 first suggested itself as a convenient one because it coincided in length with previous inquiries.[1] Monks could certainly be included, and lay rectors, and pluralist king's clerks, but not normally the higher clergy, nor the aristocracy, nor the merchants. Much has to be said of the class immediately below the gentry because they invaded Parliament, thus complicating the issue. For relatively few of the knights of the shire were 'strenuous' knights and at home some might be franklins or esquires, not *chivalers* or *milites*, though many of them were as rich as knights. As parliamentary gentry, about whom something can usually be discovered, they form part of the inquiry, and if they are gentlemen of coat armour our task is lightened. This class must, then, include franklins and esquires, and yeomen. The franklins are the yeomen of this period, the word yeoman being of later occurrence. When personal service is involved the esquire or *valettus* is the Tudor 'knave' or the French *valet*.

Population

As for the numbers concerned, we can only scratch the surface. The population in medieval England is thought to have reached a peak about 1300.[2] It was also an economic peak so far as the wool trade was concerned.[3] Out of a total estimated at between 2,500,000 and 3,000,000 people, we deal only with the adult males holding 6,000 or so knights' fees in rather less than 9,000 parishes. For a complete survey, knights on ecclesiastical estates come into view. But monks as landlords

---

[1] The period 1265–1322 was covered by the Rev. C. Moor in his list of *Knights of Edward I*, and my *History and Heraldry* was concerned with the period 1254–1310.
[2] D. Knowles, *Religious Orders*, ii. 256 n. 3, citing J. C. Russell, *British Medieval Population*.   [3] Eileen Power, *The Wool Trade* (Oxford, 1941).

must rank with the aristocracy, who often employed neighbouring gentry as lay stewards or counsellors. The 9,000 parishes, or at any rate, vills, in the *Nomina Villarum* of 1316 show that some vills had one lord, some three, depending on what part of England they lay in. On this basis we must expect to find 18,000 to 20,000 country gentry. If there were 2,000 strenuous knights only one-tenth of the gentry are knights. But the percentage varied enormously from shire to shire, and the poll-tax returns of 1381 for Yorkshire, as noted below, complete the picture. Many Yorkshire vills were without any gentry at all.

But as was remarked in another context the total number of strenuous knights was far smaller than has often been imagined. Striking confirmation of an estimate derived from the Parliamentary Roll of Arms (less the fifteenth-century additions but increased by 'swan knights' not therein mentioned), i.e. about 1,250 knights, is found in the returns of sheriffs to a muster called for 30 May 1324 at Westminster. This is something of a mystery, for the sheriffs sent up lists of knights and men-at-arms. These lists had not been asked for in the extant printed writs, which say merely that the knights are to be sent to Westminster. Presumably they did so muster to repel invasion by Roger Mortimer and Queen Isabella. In that case there could again have been 1,000 knights and some hundreds of esquires at Westminster. If this were so no one seems to have noticed the fact.[1]

The occasion must have been similar, and intended to be similar, to that earlier occasion in 1306, the Feast of the Swans, when, too, there were more than 1,000 knights in London. For one of the writs of 4 June is to the effect that all those who had £40-worth of land and had held the same for three years were to become knights by

[1] Neither the summonses for the muster nor the accompanying writs and returns are mentioned in McKisack, *The Fourteenth Century*. The matter escaped the notice of the 'Monk of Malmesbury' in *Vita Edwardi Secundi*.

THE RANKS OF SOCIETY 17

Michaelmas with horses and arms according to their estate, and each with at least a horse for himself and another. If they had only £20 in land they were to arm and mount themselves according to the Statute of Winchester—and, if less, less. And finally—and here is the interesting parallel—those who wished to receive knighthood from the King himself were to come to London before Whitsuntide (i.e. 1324) to receive their 'apparatus' from the king's wardrobe. So eighteen years after he had himself received knighthood Edward II attempted a similar occasion, possibly with his son (now aged 12) in mind, but on the suggestion of the dominating Isabella. A last writ on the subject (6 August 1324) allowed those who wished to have respite by making fine with the King to come to him on or before Michaelmas.[1]

This is not the place for a general history of these years but in fairness to Edward II it should be noticed that on his breach with Isabella he displayed a degree of activity, in organizing a fleet and munitioning castles, with which he has not always (if ever) been credited.

Three Lists (1324)

This list of knights and squires of 1324 is the completest list we have of the country gentry at this period. It gives no armorial bearings, but with the Parliamentary Roll of Arms (twelve or fifteen years earlier) behind it,

[1] A curious feature in the history of the country knights is that in 1353 men were to be distrained at the £15 level to become knights. This, in view of the change in the value of money since the occasion of Edward I, is an obvious absurdity. For, from what has already been said here and in the preceding volume, it will be clear that no one with only £15 a year in land could afford to become a knight unless he made a quite unusually favourable bargain with his lord. This needs further investigation, because taken with the summons in 1352–3 for only *one* knight from each county, it seems to indicate an acute shortage of knights for the army at that time, possibly owing to the Black Death. There is an air of unreality about this kind of distraint: it might be merely an anticipation of Stuart practice.

and Powell's Roll of c. 1350 on the other side, we have three lists invaluable for the history of this class. The 1324 list needs careful analysis. It is not at all like the P.R.A., though arranged by counties, for it was not drawn up by any central authority; it is simply a transcript of the sheriffs' returns by counties. Under each county is a list of knights followed by a list of esquires. The transcript is quite incomplete, through the mutilation of the original returns. As it is a composite document, important knights or barons are returned for as many counties as they had land in, so that there is considerable repetition. I have counted 860 knights, omitting the earls, out of 1,250 instances of knights returned. Other knights are known to have existed at this date, but the sheriffs were certainly doing their best, for they carefully included persons absent on pilgrimage or in Ireland or Gascony and the not inconsiderable number of those who were permanently unfit or over age (over 60 or about 80, according to taste). The criteria for inclusion among the esquires are not uniform. Under Cornwall we learn that all the aforesaid (does it refer to esquires only or to knights as well?) have £40 in land and rent, and under Lancashire all have £15. The question naturally arises whether the sheriffs are in fact making returns to different writs. But the same divergences of response to some urgent stimulus is seen in the *cartae* of 1164 and many another feudal inquiry.

1324 and Later Numbers

A valuable feature of this list is that in some counties the sheriff has distinguished those who resided in the county from those who were merely absentee landlords. Though this reduces the real number of knights concerned from about 1,250 to 850, it is a matter of some importance to know where a man lived, and how many knights were really available in each shire for public duties.[1]

[1] *Parl. Writs (s.a.* 1324).

THE RANKS OF SOCIETY

The total number of knights available increased again under Edward III. It has recently been shown that in 1346-7 about 950 English knights served abroad and in 1359-60 about 680 out of a total of 870.[1]

It might be expected that the *chivaler* would include knights of every kind, but in the Boroughbridge Roll the phrase *chivalers et bachelers* seems to restrict it to bannerets. This is at variance with the terminology of the returns to Parliament made by the sheriffs' offices at the same period. Knights of the shire are frequently styled *chivalers* and it is clear that they are usually if not always bachelors. When bannerets appear in Parliament it is upon summons by individual writ, like barons.[2]

Of the local men, those below the knights may be called *valetti, armigeri, scutiferi* in Latin, or *esquiers* in French, but franklins if they are free tenants, and later yeomen. This is an undifferentiated class, because some will become knights and some will not. The idea of gentility is a foreign one, coming from French or Flemish feudalism, and is appropriate only in the romantic context of the Burgundian chronicles, sumptuary legislation, and the heraldic world (as seen in the great heraldic controversy in the time of Richard II, and the Tudor heraldic visitations) as typified by Edward III and Windsor Castle, with their Round Tables, Garters, jousts, and all the trappings of continental chivalry. The idea of the English Country Gentleman cannot arise until the people have become accustomed to speak English. Indeed, by 1381, the emotional overtones of 'U' and 'non-U' are already apparent to some modern writers. But, as it happened, in the Great Revolt of 1381 it was not the

---
[1] J. W. Sherborne, 'Indentured Retinues and the English Expeditions to France', *E.H.R.* (1964), 745. This article is now the key reference on the subject.
[2] On the other hand the more normal use of the word appears in the Chauvency poem about the tournament of 1284, where, unless *chivaler* includes bannerets as well as bachelors, it would have been a tournament without bannerets.

knights so much as the lawyers and the landlords, knighted or not, who were attacked. Some of the knights were sympathetic to the movement, as Sir William Wither and his north-country friends had been to the opponents of papal exactions in the preceding century.

The mere existence of a monarchy as the fountain of honour by Divine Right, the cult of the Virgin and the Saints, supported by a secret and a foreign tongue, and above all a number of dynastic ambitions and trading interests, contrived to produce a Hundred Years War and a high time for the heralds.

Number of Knights by Counties

Northumberland is a special case, on account of the need for ceaseless watchfulness on the Scottish border. In some years they sent no members to Parliament because they were too busy defending the March[1] and dare not leave the border.[2] It cannot have been merely the distance to Westminster: it was never too much for anyone to come from Cornwall, but that is a much easier journey. It is also possible that there were few actual knights in the county, though there were undoubtedly a great many warlike folk. However, they quibbled about the matter and it was reported in 1360 that there were no knights in the county except Walter of Tynedale and he was feeble and useless.[3]

It had become very expensive to be a knight with the introduction of complete suits of plate armour, and the barding of horses.[4] The shield was rendered unnecessary.[5]

[1] No returns found for 1338. *Ret.* 1314–15, 20 Jan. to Westminster.
[2] *Ret.* 9 Sept. 1332.
[3] McKisack, *The Fourteenth Century* (1959), citing Prynne, *Brief Reg. of Parl. Writs*, iii. 166–7.   [4] A 'barded' horse is an armoured horse.
[5] The shield is last seen on the Aldeburgh, Yorks., brass of 1360. The Wantone brass of 1347 at Wimbish in Essex is the first on which the effigy bears no shield. The shield is retained for tournaments, the jousting shield having a deep notch on the dexter side for the spear. For the decorative use of heraldry see further Joan Evans, *Oxford History of English Art*, vol. v (1949).

THE RANKS OF SOCIETY

The horse's armour was covered with a brilliantly coloured textile trapper with heraldic charges as on the rider's surcoat.[1] This obligatory expense was very likely a main reason for the scarcity of knights in the later Middle Ages not only on the Scottish border but in Kent.

In a proof of age taken at Easter in 1318 it was found that Sir William de Etchingham or Echingham was the only belted knight in the whole rape of Pevensey, and that he held the barony.[2] The P.R.A. for Kent shows the names of knights about 1310, but their lands are all in Sussex.

Number of Bannerets Knights

The ratio of bannerets to knights bachelor changed considerably in the course of the fourteenth century. Fewer bannerets were created, but each led a much larger company than heretofore. So in 1337–8 for the first Breton campaign we find:

1. William Montague as banneret led 6 knights, 20 men-at-arms, 24 archers, £40 for every 40 days, the King maintaining them while in the field.
2. As newly created Earl of Salisbury, he received £2,000. 17s. 7½d. for the period 7 December 1337–13 June 1338, for himself, 1 banneret, 23 knights, 106 men-at-arms, 30 mounted archers, 56 Welsh footman, and 60 sailors. It is a simple calculation to show that the rate of pay is that generally prevailing, i.e. 4s. for a banneret *per diem*, 2s. for a bachelor, 1s. for a man-at-arms, and 6d. for an archer; and of course the Earl owed 40 days' service himself.
3. The Earl of Lancaster led 6 bannerets, 90 knights, 486 men-at-arms, and 423 mounted archers.[3]

[1] Sir James Mann, *Arms and Armour in England* (H.M. Stationery Office, 1960), 20.
[2] He died in 1326 holding 5¾ fees and one fee of Mortain (Fine Roll). See further Moor, *Knights of Edward I*, sub nomine.
[3] Bryant, *Age of Chivalry*, 303, citing *Speculum*, xix. 144.

The Local Knights in General

Edward I could get together 400 new knights very rapidly, but it had never been done before, and it was never done again.

Not only are there changes in the forms of names, but the families that matter change too. A list of country gentry provides a completely different set of prominent men in each century. The rate of change accelerates until we come to a period when a man can say 'from shirt sleeves to shirt sleeves in three generations'.

These changes are in the thirteenth and fourteenth centuries due more to the natural rise or fall of families through the personal qualities of their members, or to the failure of male heirs, than to death in war on land or at sea. The average span of military activity for the strenuous knights was fifteen years, but some few knights and many more ladies lived to a great age. The same is true of baronial families, who 'seem to have died out in the male line every third generation or so'.[1] This has been said of the fifteenth century, but is equally applicable to the fourteenth.

Knighthood was unpopular as a whole, but the class of squires[2] had by the fourteenth century for all practical purposes attained equality with that of the knights. The reluctance to serve in any public office was not, and never had been, in the gentry as a whole, but in the knights. Those immediately beneath them were only too eager to take their place. It was never difficult to get candidates for service, but it was difficult to get knights, for the knights themselves had become much more specialized in their interests. Perhaps they never really

[1] J. R. Lander, *The Wars of the Roses* (1965), cited by Raymond Mortimer in the *Sunday Times*, 24 Oct. 1965.
[2] The *valetti* of 1322 were squires, but by the mid fifteenth century *valetti* meant *yeomen* (i.e. those of 1443 whom the sheriffs were forbidden to return as knights). The squire himself, at that time *armiger*, was on the way to becoming *the squire* of the village, the unofficial lord of the place.

THE RANKS OF SOCIETY 23

wanted to serve, but they had to obey the wishes of a powerful and politically shrewd King, whose wrath was terrible. Edward II did not care, and Edward III could manage just as well with the squires.

Franklins

If we confine ourselves to the dictionary definitions there will be difficulty in delimiting our subject, which in the thirteenth century was covered by the chivalry or knights, that is everyone from the king downwards who was a person of coat armour. Already by 1310 there was a class of non-armigerous persons of the same families, rank, and wealth. The style 'country gentry' seemed to cover them all. If we jump to the time of Richard II we find quite another state of affairs. We are trying to describe the kind of men who administered the countryside, and we turned naturally to the knights of the shire and burgesses. The knights of the shire in some cases ceased to be knights before the Lords and Commons became separate houses.

Long before the end of the Middle Ages 'the gentry' have come to mean, for the heralds, the class immediately below the knights. The esquires or *armigeri* began by bearing quite literally the arms of their lords or knights they served. By the time of the lost roll of Sir Robert Laton (1370), which appears in the great Scrope–Grosvenor controversy (1385), in the Court of Chivalry, coats of arms were borne by lords, knights, and esquires. This occurs at the end of our chosen period, and thereafter books of 'Who's Who' at any given periods will include peerage, baronage, knightage, and gentry. One of the early English notables, apart from London aldermen, whose arms as an esquire are recorded is Geoffrey Chaucer, who when he was not a Londoner lived the life of a country gentleman in Somerset and Kent. He was in 1367 and 1372–3 variously described as a *valettus* or yeoman of the king's chamber, and in 1372–3 as *armiger*, *scutifer*, or esquire, and as such he bore *per pale argent and gules, a bend countercharged*. He was a 'strenuous' man who had seen considerable military service in the field. The Black Prince's follower Sir Dietrich Van Dale had a similar career. The *cursus honorum* for a man who had very considerable responsibilities was esquire, yeoman, bachelor. Chaucer seems to have been quite content to remain a king's squire.

By the time of the poll tax of 1380 and the Peasants' Revolt of 1381 the definition has ceased to cover the subject. For we are told that the franklins are the class immediately below the gentry and in the poll-tax returns for the West Riding of Yorkshire of 1379 the franklins are assessed at 3*s*. 4*d*. and the knights at 20*s*.[1] So the franklin is 'one sixth of a knight'. Yet Chaucer's franklin had sat in Parliament and had been sheriff. It appears from Chaucer that even if they had no title by blood to gentility or chivalry they might (at any rate when on pilgrimage) be socially acceptable. It has always been a literary convention that franklins and yeomen, including of course archers, are honest folk, who speak English, while barons, bannerets, and more so baronets are black-hearted ruffians, and, by preference, talk French.[2]

The franklin, who has no place in a French-speaking court, is the late-thirteenth- and fourteenth-century equivalent of the later yeoman farmer. He is much in evidence in the records of the lay subsidy of 1379. From these we learn that in the West Riding of Yorkshire the franklin was on the same financial level as the squire. The knights in this invaluable social document number only a dozen out of a total 20,000 men, women, and children over 14 or 15. Perhaps we might say, for Yorkshire, one country gentleman to every 500 grown men.

[1] G. T. Clark, F.S.A., *Y.A.J.* viii (1882), 6, 145, 169. The Suffolk returns will be found in E. Powell, *The Rising in East Anglia* (Cambridge, 1896).

[2] Frankleyn appears as a surname about 1325 in Oxon. and Somerset. (*C. Cl. R.*, Index.)

THE RANKS OF SOCIETY

The number of these men who fought at Crécy and Poitiers remains highly controversial. M. Ferdinand Lot gives the English 6,000 men all told at Poitiers and the French 5,000 to 6,000. Colonel A. H. Burne disagrees, and nearly all contemporary writers say that the French were much more numerous than the English. In view of the relative sizes and resources of the two countries, it may be felt that Colonel Burne is likely to be right.[1]

The phraseology of the royal court becomes stereotyped, outdated, and misleading so far as the shires are concerned. Chaucer's franklin[2] becomes the model for Macauley's squire—'his table was loaded with coarse plenty'. Franklins are never found at court and have so to speak disappeared or become yeomen. The only distinction between them and the squires in the fourteenth century was that the franklins, yeomen, bowmen, or free tenants did not aspire to become knights. The squire, at whatever date, or however poor, was born within the charmed circle or had achieved enough by his exertions to be so admitted. He could become part of the establishment, but his place in society fluctuated almost from generation to generation.

The terminology of the lesser royal households, particularly that of the Black Prince, is that of the court, so that the *cursus honorum* could run squire–yeoman–knight bachelor, but in real life, and using the words in their modern sense, the feudal squire did not become a yeoman, who was socially beneath him, nor did the yeoman become a squire.[3]

The terminology of the chivalrous class offers no great difficulty in the thirteenth or fourteenth century in so far

---

[1] See A. H. Burne, *The Crécy War* (London, 1955), 312–16.

[2] *Canterbury Tales: The Prologue*, ll. 339–48. The only chronicle evidence for the word franklin seems to be in Robert of Gloucester's Chronicle (R.S. 1887), p. 61, and the Chronicle of Robert of Brunne (R.S. 1887), l. 6547.

[3] *B.P.R.* iv, s.v. Sir Dietrich van Dale. The subject has been thoroughly bedevilled by the adoption in the 1890s by the P.R.O. of this quite artificial terminology. The calendars of chancery records are full of king's yeomen, etc., who never existed.

as bannerets, bachelors, or esquires are concerned. All these persons are within the charmed circle: they are gentlemen of coat armour, and whether at court or not their social standing is not in doubt. Once we leave this restricted class a distinction has to be made between the terminology of the court and that of the shires. For there were always many well-born persons at court who performed often in person for the king and queen or their children, or the prince's children or the duke's children, many services that in lesser households would be regarded as menial. Thus a yeoman at court and a yeoman farmer, or, in the period covered by this book, a franklin, are hardly on the same social level.

The equation that makes a yeoman the equivalent of a valet comes from a well-known petition of 1363.[1] The yeomen (*valetti*) of the central government are the *scutiferi* or *armigeri* in the shires. All these words imply household or personal service.

The official translation of this statute of 1363 is particularly unfortunate in that the later yeomen, the 'yeomen of England', are usually thought of as particularly independent people. But as the style yeoman hardly occurs in the contemporary records of this period it need not detain us. The word did not become generalized until the fifteenth century and later, and still survives in the Yeomen of the Guard. The men styled yeomen in the thirteenth and fourteenth centuries did 'yeoman service' no doubt. The yeomen (if the *valetti* are to be so styled) of Edward I's household could be rich men, and a high percentage of them came from chivalrous families. They were unwarlike men, professionals at their jobs, but not clerks in Holy orders. They were feodaries, cooks, castellans, purveyors to the household, masons, or surveyors. As such they are often styled Mr. like Mr. Richard Raven,

[1] 37 Ed. III capp. 8–15 (in Rot. Parl. (1777), ii. 278–81), cited by Mildred Campbell, 'Early Usage of the Word Yeoman', *The English Yeoman*, App. I, 389–94. This Yale University study is very clear and well put.

THE RANKS OF SOCIETY

yeoman, the Black Prince's master cook, or Robert de Eleford, the Prince's yeoman, steward of his lands in Devon and Cornwall and sheriff of Cornwall at £40 per annum, in succession to John Dabernoun.[1] The pay is equivalent to that of a knight bachelor. The work of such yeomen must have demanded a certain level of literacy. Though *magister* alone is insufficient evidence of a master's degree, it may still point to a mate's ticket.[2] An important but typical king's yeoman was Matthew de Columbers, a highly successful London merchant, who in 1278 was appointed as Chamberlain, king's butler and coroner, an office usually by deputy in the city of London,[3] and to the gaugership of wines in the realm. He received the issues of his office and accounted at the Exchequer, in return for twenty marks a year, which was more than the fee of a king's banneret at that time. The grant was extended from time to time, and on 6 January 1281 it was made a life appointment, extended to Ireland in 1282, the year of his death. By that grant he was to receive the issues for his maintenance, in addition to his fee of twenty marks.[4]

The main line of the family is represented by the Matthew who is No. 190 on Glover's roll bearing *argent, a chief gules*, who, since he bears the same arms as William de Fors de Vivonia, might be thought to have been of Poitevin descent, but Colombers is in Lorraine. This Michael married Matilda. They held lands in Hampshire and the manor of Pipardesclive in Wiltshire. On his death in 1282 he left an heir, Michael.[5] The Matthew of 1290 may be a younger son or a cousin. There was an

[1] *B.P.R.* (Cornwall), 62 (18 Aug. 1354).
[2] The mate of a merchant ship is always addressed as Mister. Cf. the frequency of 'good master' so-and-so. The word is still used in widely different contexts.
[3] In 1290 his son and heir Michael (d. 19 March 1291) had an indemnity for his coroners not doing their duty in London.
[4] *C. Cl. R.* (1282), 145, is a key reference. See also the *Liber Custumarum* (R.S.) and *C.P.R.* (1278), 269, 272, 360; (1282), 29, 361.
[5] *C. Cl. R.* (1282), 161, and *The Genealogist*, xxi. 25.

indemnity to him in this year for his coroners not doing their duty in London.[1] Part of the interest of this career lies in the history of the de Vere chamberlainship, for it might be thought to be Robert de Vere's business not the King's to appoint deputies throughout the realm. That this was not so is shown by the Lord Edward's own appointment as chamberlain of Sandwich on 6 March 1268, at a time when he was accumulating offices at Westminster and in the provinces prior to his crusade. It seems possible that Edward treated the chamberlainship as he had already treated the stewardship, a policy facilitated by the behaviour of his Grand Chamberlain, Robert de Vere, Earl of Oxford.

These hereditary household officials made nothing but trouble. Robert de Vere,[2] as an active supporter of Simon de Montfort, had forfeited his lands in 1265. He is said to have been restored soon after,[3] and he lived until 1296. But we do not know whether he was restored with the right of appointing deputies at court or elsewhere. This would account for Edward's appointment as chamberlain at Sandwich in 1268 and the appearance of a king's knight as Chamberlain throughout the realm in 1278.

Matthew had been one of the Lord Edward's trusted servants. It was he and three other king's knights (or possibly bannerets) who had been put in charge as keepers of the peace in the Isle of Wight on 21 August 1267[4] when the Lady of the Isle had shown sympathy for de Montfort and openly abetted his party.[5]

[1] *C.P.R.* (1290), 361.
[2] The Vere of 1142 was Count of Guisnes, and this helps to explain the appearance of a Count of Guisnes on some rolls of arms.
[3] *Handbook of British Chronology*.
[4] The other three are perhaps better known—Alan Plugenet, Reynaud de Molis, and Ralph de Gorges, all south-country men and among the Lord Edward's inner circle. Matthew de Columbers was a tenant of the Lady of the Isle (Isabella de Fortibus, dowager Countess of Aumale and Devon). He occurs in P.R.O. Min. Acct. 1118/22 (an account roll of the Oxfordshire manor of Whitchurch for 1281-2), and he or his father attested a charter of the Countess to Lacock Abbey in 1265.   [5] *C.P.R.* 156.

THE RANKS OF SOCIETY 29

There is much that is obscure in this story, but it illustrates the difficulty of accepting 'king's yeoman' as an adequate description of Matthew's status. A considerable number of king's yeomen, probably all, were of the armigerous class, e.g. in 1272–9 they included a Fitz-Warin, a DePlessetis, two Lestranges, a Felton, and Gui Ferre. Columbers remained a king's yeoman to the end of his life, and is an excellent example of the lack of accord between the terminology of the court and that of provincial life.

Local Disorder

At first sight there does not seem to be much difference between the amount of disorder in England as between the period of the three Edwards (if we begin only in the last decade of the thirteenth century) and the fifteenth century, which is much better documented. More vivid pictures are presented by private letters in French or English than by Chancery enrolments in Latin, which may have to magnify or seem to magnify a breach of the peace to bring it within the meaning of some legal formula. In the later period the bands of retainers were much larger, and someone gave names not only to the battles but to the period.

The first period of disorder lasts from the failure of Edward I to maintain a war on two or even three fronts simultaneously. It really begins with Edward I's personal and domestic tragedies of 1290–2, the loss of Burnell, his great Chancellor, the Queen Mother, and his devoted wife. The beginnings of this period, the breakdown of the older systems for keeping the peace and the tentative steps taken to find a better method, have been briefly touched upon in an earlier book.[1] The fifteenth-century disorders have long been a subject of study fascinating in detail, dismal in the round.

[1] *History and Heraldry.*

The gang riots of the intervening period, from the loss of Gascony or the confiscation thereof in 1294 to the outbreak of full-scale war under Edward III in 1337, have more recently been studied,[1] but if the Close and Patent Rolls are a safe guide there is much to be done before the subject can be treated as a whole. As soon as we dig below the surface in any county it appears to be crawling with miscreants, robbers, renegade clergy, faithless knights, and rascals of every complexion—king's men gone wrong or Lancastrians without a master. The political ineptitude of Edward II plus a certain bloody-minded obstinacy combined with the ambitious and treacherous incapacity of Earl Thomas, who could not recognize his own limitations, to give a most unpleasant flavour to the political omelettes of the period. Most of the local disorders had no political significance at all: they were due simply to 'lack of governance' or abuse of authority, occasionally to 'vaulting ambition'; more frequently the troubles were incidents in a long-standing feud with neighbours. When the central government is weak, that is the signal for looting and rioting and even crying 'Havoc', though in each case there will be some immediate local grievance.

The wickedness of notorious 'malfeasers and maintainers',[2] and of champertors (*campi participes*) who divided among themselves the profits of a lawsuit that they had illegally 'maintained' in court, was the subject of a number of statutes, beginning with the *ordinacio de Conspiratoribus* of 1305 (Trailbaston). M. Jusserand gave a vivid account of one of these 'organized and quasi-seignorial bands' many years ago,[3] concerning the Shropshire knights and others who successfully ambushed the servants of a rich merchant.

[1] J. G. Bellamy, 'The Coterel Gang: An Anatomy of a Band of Fourteenth-Century Criminals,' in *E.H.R.* (1964), 698–717.
[2] Stat. 10 Edward III, A.D. 1336.
[3] J. J. Jusserand, *English Wayfaring Life in the Middle Ages*, 3rd edn. (1925), 150–3. The knights concerned were Sir Robert de Ridewere and Sir John de Oddyngseles.

THE RANKS OF SOCIETY

The obvious answer to this prevalence of local disorder was the fortification and crenellation of country houses, and these can be plotted on a map. The two cannot be expected to coincide. Castles are built for the avoidance of trouble, not to create it, and perhaps Robin Hood and his Sherwood foresters would have found immortality in monkish chronicles rather than in popular ballads but for the geographical propinquity of Nottingham Castle.

The better-known instances of local disorder in Edward II's reign were Gilbert de Middleton's attack in 1317 on the Cardinals in Yorkshire,[1] the activities of the Folevilles of Ashby Foleville in Leicestershire,[2] and those of the Coterel confederacy in Derbyshire (1328–33).[3] There are also numerous examples of similar activities that merge into private war, such as the doings of Adam Banastre in Lancashire and of Payn Turbervile and Llewellyn Bren in Glamorgan, but this is rebellion against the king, not gang warfare. At the same time as Earl Warenne in Yorkshire was waging a private war, there were riots at Bristol, and William de Somerton, Prior of Binham, was in armed rebellion against the mother house of St. Albans.[4]

Fortunately for the country, the forces of disorder did not attempt to coalesce on the invasion of Queen Isabella in 1326, which resulted in the overthrow of the King. The loyalty of the rank and file of the civil service to their work, including the Prince's household, was admirable,

---

[1] McKisack, *The Fourteenth Century*, 40–1, and my *The 'Liber Epistolaris' of Richard de Bury*, 81.

[2] E. L. G. Stones, 'The Folevilles of Ashby Foleville and their Associates in Crime', *T.R.H.S.* (1957), 117–36. This was an official family. John de Foleville had been a king's banneret in 1286, and he or a namesake was knight of the shire for Rutland in 1298, 1301; Leics. 1301 (i.e. both counties that year) 1300, 1302, and 1306. He bore *barry wavy of six Argent and Sable, a quarter Gules* (Collins 526). Ralph de Foleville was Knight of the shire for Leics. 1315. It was Eustace especially who led the gang about 1330.

[3] J. G. Bellamy, 'The Coterel Gang: an Anatomy of a Band of Fourteenth-Century Criminals', *E.H.R.* (1964), 698–717.

[4] For Adam Banastre and Llewellyn Bren and the riots at Bristol see *Vita Edwardi*, 64–9, etc. For William de Somerton see W. J. Smith in *E.H.R.* lxix (1954), 78–83, and my *The 'Liber Epistolaris' of Richard de Bury*, 109.

and the transference of power prepared by the manœuverings of some politically minded bishops, notably Orleton of Hereford, was effected without much bloodshed; except in London, where Bishop Stapledon of Exeter was murdered. There was nowhere any loyalty to Edward II. One at least of his own household, Sir John Maltravers, was prepared to act as his gaoler. This was a key man in every sense, as he had been steward of the royal household.

Castles and their importance

Many of the country gentry spent part of their time on garrison duty in a neighbouring castle, or as members of its permanent staff in official meetings there. For the uses of a royal or baronial castle extended far beyond its military function. In the social and administrative life of the shire the castle played a part still seen in Elizabethan times at Kenilworth, just as the old regime survived in some of its former splendour for the 'castle folk' of nineteenth-century Dublin. Only in the monastery or the castle could the amenities that a herald would naturally desire, be found, and there it was that the painted rolls were probably made. In making a roll of arms the herald would turn to the sheriff's office in the castle, for it was here that he could obtain a sight of the muster rolls made up by the Marshal's deputy. So it is that occasional rolls could be made here, though tournament rolls would be made on the spot, not painted at leisure, since it was the heralds themselves who marshalled the tournaments, the Round Tables, and the jousts.

The castles of our period were less important as military strongpoints—except the big strategic ones on the coast and on the borders of Wales and Scotland—than as centres of administration. Seignorial as well as royal, they had always been local receipts,[1] and they were the

---

[1] For the castles as local receipts under King John see J. E. A. Jolliffe's article in *Essays presented to Frederick Maurice Powicke* (1948). The great

THE RANKS OF SOCIETY

administrative centres for the districts upon which they depended for their food supplies. It was there that the accounts of officials were audited, courts held, and records kept. If the castle went with the county, as it did in Northamptonshire, it or a neighbouring royal house was also the county record office, and the shire court would hold its sessions very near the records, in charge perhaps of the under-sheriff or the clerk of the county court. In Berkshire they would be in the shire hall at Reading. In Caernarvon, at first in the Chamberlain's Tower in the castle, and in our period in Shire Hall Street, where the gaol was. At Oxford, too, the archives and gaol were in the castle, at the bottom of George Street. At Norwich in 1326 the king's house called the Shirehous was ordered to be rebuilt and all royal ministers appointed to take assizes, juries, certificates, and inquisitions, and to deliver gaols to hold their sessions there and not elsewhere.[1] This would include coroners, escheators, and commissioners of array.

The castle or the shire hall was the only permanent local repository known to have been available to constables and marshals, so therefore the castle or shire hall could accommodate a muster-roll or any nominal roll not required to be returned at once to Westminster, or (1332-7) to York.

There is a problem here that still awaits solution, for the first line of the Caerlaverock poem states that the writer has *found in the chronicles of great musters*—a singularly tantalizing phrase, as the muster for that campaign was at Carlisle (25 June 1300), unless the herald was already in close touch with the army. It is possible to suppose that the poem was fashioned either at Caerlaverock itself after the siege, when Clifford was in

taxes on movables of 1225 and 1232 were also stored in provincial castles. The vital role of castles on the Fortibus estates is fully explained in my *Seignorial Administration in England* (1937), as regards Cockermouth, Skipton, and Carisbrooke Castles.

[1] *Cal. Cl. R.* (4 Feb. 1326), 415, 444.

charge, or at his own castle of Appleby in Westmorland (seventy-five miles to the south), of which he was hereditary sheriff. If his own herald-minstrel was involved he would have access to any documents there. Cooke's Ordinary,[1] too, has some connection with the county court of Carmarthen, but that is a tangled story, and Glover's roll possibly has some link with Kenilworth Castle, which went with the counties of Leicester and Warwick. The final solution may be that the Boroughbridge roll was not made when it appears to have been made.[2]

The homes of the military class: country houses and crenellation

Few country houses have survived from the fourteenth century or earlier to the present day, and not a great many castles.[3] The latter are usually royal castles. The best-preserved manor house of the period is said to be Little Wenham Hall in Suffolk (*c.* 1270–80). At Little Chesterford in Essex there is a stone building with timber-framed aisled hall (*c.* 1320 or later) with fifteenth-century added left wing.[4] King John's house at Warnford in Hampshire (early thirteenth century); and the Charney Basset manor house in Berkshire, which consisted of a hall and solar and a separate kitchen.[5] The danger of fire was the reason for this last feature, which continued for centuries, and is seen in a modified fifteenth-century form at Magdalen College, Oxford. Another that survived is Penshurst in Sussex, the original home of Sir Stephen de Penchester, Constable of

---

[1] *Infra*, pp. 9, 34, 97 ff.
[2] *Infra*, p. 76.
[3] See in general, and for other surviving houses, Bannister Flelcher, *A History of Architecture on the Comparative Method*, 17th edn. revised (1965) by R. A. Cordingley, 437–514; and Margaret Wood, *The English Medieval House 1066–1540* (Country Life Publications, 1965).
[4] *Medieval Essex* (County Council Publications, 2nd edn. 1964).
[5] H. A. Tipping, *English Homes* (London, 1921–37); Period (I): 1066–1487.

Dover Castle.[1] The coheiress of Roger de Lascelles in 1323 inherited at Kirby Knole in the North Riding a mansion consisting of hall with pantry, buttery, and a chamber on the north; stable and garden; kitchen, brewhouse, and bakehouse under one roof; knights' chamber, gatehouse, barn, watermill, and windmill.[2]

Some country houses were fortified, and as this could only be done by royal licence, usually known as a licence to crenellate, more is known about them.[3] The right to control fortifications does not rest upon statute, as Stubbs points out.[4] It is a matter of ancient prerogative and thus needs royal licence.[5] Such licences are extant from the time of Henry III onwards, and a large number were collected from the patent rolls by Mr. J. H. Parker of Oxford for Stubbs, who summarizes his results as follows:[6] twenty licences between 1257 and 1273; forty-four *temp.* Edward I; fifty-eight *temp.* Edward III (*recte* II); one hundred and eighty *temp.* Edward III. The evidence collected by Mr. J. H. Parker, of *Domestic Architecture* fame, points to an increasing feeling of insecurity in the countryside, but no one with any knowledge of the *Tempus Turbacionis* and the disruption of local government in the period of baronial reform and revolution could have deduced these phenomena from the statistics given.

[1] Penchester in 1271 had licence to crenellate his house at Hever (*History and Heraldry*, 77–8).
[2] *C. Cl. R.* (1323), 33.
[3] Ripley Castle, Yorks., was little more than a hall, probably built by Sir Thomas Ingleby, Justice of King's Bench, *Temp.* Ed. III. It is not in Parker's list of licences to crenellate. St. Donat's Castle, Glam. (*c.* 1300), is a fortified dwelling on a spur of high ground commanding the Bristol Channel, the property of Sir Peter Stradling, and latterly a depository for the collections of antiques by the late Mr. Randolph Hearst, the American newspaper owner.
[4] W. Stubbs, *The Constitutional History of England*, 3rd edn. (1884), iii. 554, § 442, 472, Chap. XXI, citing Mr. Parker in the *Gentleman's Magazine*, N.S. I (1856), 208 seq.
[5] The Commons petitioned for the right in 1371 (*Rot. Parl.* II. 307).
[6] Mr. Parker searched the chancery rolls for licences to crenellate as one of the preliminary labours towards his *History of Domestic Architecture*, which brought him an honorary M.A., and he became the first keeper of the post at the Ashmolean Museum that he himself endowed (see the *D.N.B.*).

Parker did not use the close rolls, only a few addenda of licences under Privy Seal. Hence he missed the fluctuating attitude of the government to Roger Leyburne and the castle built by him in Kent in the 1260s, and he missed seven others from the patent rolls up to 1273.

Like any other medieval licence (e.g. mortmain), a licence to crenellate would be granted to any applicant if he was not openly hostile to the crown, and could afford it. Even foreign merchants resident in London, or having a house there, could obtain a licence, as did the well-known Cahorsin merchant William Servat.[1] The bulk of the licences went to the religious houses, the bishops, and other royal clerks, like John Benstede of Rosemont at Eye (1307); to a professional M.P. like Constantine de Mortimer of Sculton in Norfolk (1322–3), or to important knights like the Scropes and the Constables of Flamborough in Yorkshire. Most of the baronage were already safely established in their castles.

Though these converted country houses are referred to when crenellated as castles, it is not to be imagined that anyone but a very rich man could afford a real castle. In some cases only a wooden superstructure is mentioned, in others a wall of stakes. If you surrounded your house with a moat, you had a castle, and a licence became necessary. Eight royal castles in Wales cost £80,000 in five to seven seasons (April to November each year), half the money and much of the labour coming from Ireland. Two to three thousand men were employed.[2] No earl except Gloucester, Richard of Cornwall (who would not have

---

[1] See my 'Caversins and Merchants of Cahors', *Medievalia et Humanistica* (1946), revised edn. in *Collected Papers* ii, (forthcoming). See also *C.P.R.* (1305), 379. A similar system of licences operated in Gascony, but more strictly, e.g. Charles Figeac, i. 375 (ex rot. Gasc. 26 Aug. 1290), permission to fortify a manor, but so that the tenant find security *de manerio illo nobis reddendo iratus et pacatus secundum legem* [MS. *regem*] *et consuetudinem parcium illarum*.

[2] J. G. Edwards, 'Castle-Building in Wales' *Proc. Brit. Acad.* for 1946 (publ. 1951), especially 15–81.

THE RANKS OF SOCIETY

been interested anyway), or Thomas of Lancaster and his successor Henry, or the Black Prince could (up to *c.* 1370) spend money on this scale.

The local distribution of these licences for fortified buildings shows that Yorkshire was consistently in the lead with 35 licences spread over the period 1260–1377. Kent is next with 15, Northumberland 14, Sussex 12, London and Middlesex 14, Shropshire 9 (including Walter Langton and John Charlton), Cumberland 10, thus revealing anxiety over Scottish raids or French raids. It may be thought surprising that Devon has 11. (Perhaps it had something to do with disturbances caused by smugglers or pirates?) Why there should be 10 each in Northamptonshire and Norfolk is uncertain, but it seems to point to the prevalence of local disorder in these counties on a greater scale or of more frequent occurrence than in other counties. Few firm conclusions can be drawn from the evidence because it should be correlated with the location and spheres of influence of existing royal or great baronial castles. For example Kenilworth Castle perhaps had its *contado* like any Italian town, but the nature of the influence would depend upon the tenant. The sheriff's fine stronghold at Nottingham was counterbalanced by the proximity of Sherwood forest, and its not always legendary outlaws. The subject is ripe for a topographical display of the evidence, with royal and baronial castles and crenellated houses plotted upon a map, perhaps superimposed upon the Ordnance Survey Map of Medieval England. The evidence has long been available. For the purposes of this book two such maps would be sufficient—one showing the situation in 1310 and the other England and Wales in 1377. A single map in two colours could be made to suffice if necessary, with, for example, all the castles prior to 1310 in red and the fourteenth-century licences up to 1377 in blue.

In spite of the social disasters of the mid fourteenth century the knights and gentry of the period lived in increasing comfort in these country houses, crenellated or not. From that time until Shakespeare bequeathed his second-best bed by will, a good bed was one of the marks of a gentleman, and after his horses and armour (if any) one of his most valued possessions. Sir John Cavendish the judge (d. 1381) had one powdered with popinjays, and Simon Burley of Herefordshire (d. 1388), the royal favourite, left one of green tartaryn, embroidered with ships and birds.[1] Another such extravagant bed was owned by the Earl of Oxford in 1388.[2]

Corrodars

Edward I's civil servants were well treated in their old age. Some, like John de Cobham (1300) and Peter de Leicester (1301), barons of the exchequer, or Philip de Willoughby, Dean of Lincoln and Chancellor of the Exchequer (1301), received the unusual privilege of retiring from court and dwelling in their own houses 'for rest, recreation, or on private business', and returning to their work as and when they pleased, or if the king sent for them.[3] Others, like Mr. Robert de Wyvile, was sent to Worcester Abbey as a corrodar in 1299.[4] Henry de Munpellers, a king's sergeant and London merchant, was to be received with one horse and groom at Westminster.[5] Most of them may be assumed to have settled down happily, but it was not always so. John of Coventry, the royal clerk for many years under Edward I and Edward II, was sent to Ramsey Abbey, and the monks provided him

[1] *D.N.B.*, s.v.
[2] M. V. Clarke, *Fourteenth-Century Studies* (Oxford, 1937), 116–17.
[3] *C.P.R.* 485, 615.
[4] *Ann. Wigorn*, 542. Cf. The *'Liber Epistolarie'* of *Richard de Bury*, No. 417.
[5] *C.P.R.* (1302–7), 188 (Mar. 1303). The subject is well worth investigation but only a few instances are indexed in the 1296–1302 volume of the *C. Cl. R.* and none at all in the next volume (1302–7), though there are 14 on pp. 76–7.

with food and clothing and a chamber as one of their clerks for many years, but 'afterwards they withdrew successively certain portions of his maintainance', and eventually expelled him for no crime. Nothing further is known of him.[1]

The early history of Sir Thomas de Banbury, Kt., has not come down to us. He might be described as a knight errant in search of a corrody, for he served Edward I and II faithfully and was sent to Holy Trinity Priory, Canterbury, but the monks refused to have him. That was in 1310. In March 1311 he was rebuffed from Burton-on-Trent, and on 5 October 1311 the bailiff in England of Fecamp Abbey also turned him away.[2]

It was these corrodars who in the thirteenth and fourteenth centuries did much to maintain the tradition of literary activity among retired civil servants,[3] though the wealthier ones like Richard de Bury or Chaucer needed no such assistance. Of the many others, Thomas de Wykes and Philip of Eye were at Oseney Abbey by Oxford in the last year of Henry III's reign.[4] It now seems to me that the 'Monk of Malmesbury', the chronicler who according to Stubbs 'could hardly have been a monk', could very well have been a corrodar of the abbey of which he was a neighbour and a tenant, and whence the lost manuscript of his chronicle certainly derived.[5] If Mr. Walwayn wrote it, as I have elsewhere suggested, he would not have been a royal corrodar because he was in disgrace for incompetence as Treasurer of England, but on failure of the royal bounty he could easily have arranged a corrody for himself, as his predecessor Philip of Eye had done at Oseney,

[1] *C. Cl. R.* (1323), 430.
[2] The Banbury arms are on P.R.A. (Oxon.) 338 as a fifteenth-century addition.
[3] Cf. T. F. Tout, 'The Civil Service in the Fourteenth Century', in his *Collected Papers*.
[4] 'Thomas de Wykes and his Chronicle', *E.H.R.* (May 1946).
[5] 'The Authorship of the *Vita Edwardi Secundi*', *E.H.R.* (1956). This was an odd lapse on the part of Stubbs and a still worse one on mine.

though the idea did not present itself to Stubbs, nor, until recently, to myself.¹

¹ Malmesbury was a royal abbey, and the king had sent a corrodar there in 1323 to replace another who had died (William le Engleys in place of Philip Artois. See *C. Cl. R.* (2 Nov. 1323), 142). Edward sent a king's sergeant to Bridlington the same year (ibid. 162). As he is No. 384 on Collins's roll he was presumably at Dunbar in 1296 and on the Caerlaverock campaign (Galloway roll No. 18). The rest of the story is in the *C. Cl. R.* under the dates mentioned in the text.

II

THE KNIGHTS IN THE FOURTEENTH CENTURY

THERE were only two ranks of knighthood before the foundation of the Order of the Garter. The Garter Knights were bannerets, but they were men set apart by this unique honour, the envy of all Christendom.

There were no longer any knights errant roaming the countryside seeking adventures, offering to break a lance with any chivalrous person they might encounter, but the type persisted in the more formalized wanderings of men like Sir Giles de Argentine,[1] and in the later stages of the war opportunity enough was offered by the Free Companies.

There were special household knights called king's knights (bannerets and bachelors) in the royal household, and the equivalent in private households, without any special designation, though we came near, I believe, to having Knights of the Swan in 1306, in anticipation of the Garter; and the *commilitones* might easily have become a fraternity or brotherhood as often happened later on the continent, or in the monastic world. All these household knights were like any other local knights apart from the badges or insignia that they shared with their lord's non-resident retainers. These would be serving by indenture or contract and on call in case of war, and sometimes tournament. In the thirteenth century they were often called strenuous knights.[2]

---

[1] See Appendix I.

[2] An important problem to which the answer is extremely elusive for this period is how much time knights in retainer spent with their lords and how much on their own manor. If their service was for castle guard or war and tournaments only, the answer is simple. As for the rest it seems that their lives

There were also many professional men, such as sheriffs, stewards, feodaries, some constables, high-court judges, and J.P.s, and some officials of the central government, e.g. the wardrobers, who led the household knights. This is a considerable class of men (many of them Buzones) who in one way or another devoted their lives to local administration or the judicature. The local government of the country rested largely on their shoulders from the thirteenth century until the nineteenth. The most responsible and interesting part of their work was in Parliament.[1]

As an example of king's knights and king's clerks, the Kendal family are apposite. They belong to that small class of wardrobe, later chamber, officials who did so much of the work of government, and in their day were probably almost as important as Droxford or Benstede. The number of king's knights and king's bannerets does not seem to have varied greatly.[2] In 1330 there were 26 bannerets, 43 knights, and 114 esquires who received robes at court, but in 1334 the numbers were only 9, 27, and 79. There is no particular significance in these numbers, though they give some indication of the size of the court that the king liked to have around him.[3] The apparent decrease just at the time when Edward III was preparing for his maximum effort against the Scots can only mean that more king's knights and esquires were being employed outside court. It will be remembered that in 1298 there were 44 bannerets in the king's brigade at Falkirk.

must have followed a pattern very similar to that of officers in the Royal Navy or the Indian Frontier Force at a much later date.

[1] Some of the lords of parliament were not barons but bannerets, as for example Chandos. See Tout, Chap. III, 296 n. 1, and *Collected Papers* (Manchester, 1934), ii. 180.

[2] The use of the words king's knight and king's banneret drops out of the chancery enrolments, as calendared, almost completely in Edward II's reign.

[3] Exch. Accts. 385/4 cited in *The English Government at Work, 1327–1336*, ii. 217. The author of this chapter did not realize that the minstrels included kings of arms.

The Kendal Family

The family of Kendal were presumably tenants of the barony of Kendal in Westmorland, which is mentioned in 1335 on the close roll, apparently as belonging to Margaret de Ros of Hamlake. It was erected into an earldom in 1389 for John of Lancaster, the third son of Henry IV. The family that derived its name from Kendal is first prominent from the heraldic point of view in the P.R.A. and owed its rise to two men, Hugh and Robert.[1]

Three members of this remarkable family rose from obscurity in 1272 to positions of considerable responsibility under Edward I and Edward II as king's clerks and king's knights. The earliest and most important was Hugh de Kendal, of whom more below.

Robert de Kendal was knighted at the Feast of the Swans in 1306.[2] In 1310 when he was Warden of the Cinque Ports and Constable of Dover,[3] he was at the first Dunstable tournament in the Earl of Warwick's retinue (No. 67). At least five other members of the family appear on the rolls of arms at this period, and as M.P.s for Westmorland (1318), Shropshire (1319), and Hertfordshire (1336). There is an Edmund in Northumberland and Cumberland about 1310 and an Edmund who is the Black Prince's bachelor as Steward of Cornwall, Wallingford, and other Duchy lands.

Hugh appears as a chancery clerk acting in various executive capacities from 1275,[4] as a keeper of vacant

[1] *D.N.B.* has nothing relevant to the Kendals until Charles II's Duchess of Kendal.   [2] Ashmole's list, No. 71.

[3] The Constables of Dover up to 1309 will be found in *History and Heraldry*. Robert de Kendal occurs from 1310 in *Cal. Chancery Warrants*. He was a knight in Hants, Beds., and Herts. in 1324 (*Parl. Writs*), but was dead in Mar. 1336, as was his son and heir Edward (*C. Cl. R.* 659), whose arms were *Argent a bend Vert a label Gules* (2 Dunst. 31 = Ashm. roll 15A, No. 180 and Cotgrave No. 340, P.R.A. (Herts.) 404). Robert bore the same. For John Kendall, Richard III's secretary and Keeper of the Signet, see P. M. Kendall, *Richard the Third*, cited in his *The Yorkist Age*, 313.

[4] His name occurs from 1273 in connection with small debts in *C. Cl. R.* 45, 247, also as a king's clerk from 1275, and as keeper of Vacancies in 1275 (See

benefices and in connection with coinage offences and the goods of condemned Jews.[1] By 1280 he was a clerk of the royal household, living with his brother Peter near St. Martin's church, free from the interference of the king's billeting officers, harbingers, or marshals.[2] In 1281 he was attorney for Peter de Champvent, later Steward of the Household, who was going overseas.[3]

By this time Chancery is largely 'out of court' and often a long distance from the king and his household. As a senior chancery clerk and clerk of the household Hugh is perhaps a liaison officer between the household of the king and the household of the Chancery. He ended his career junior to William de Hamilton,[4] but senior to John Langton,[5] and much business was at times done by Chancery on his authority as Keeper of the Seal (1283–4) while the king was busy with the war in North Wales,[6] and at other times while Burnell had retired to Acton Burnell in Shropshire.[7]

The explanation of this double life seems to be found in two surviving wardrobe accounts for the years 1285 and 1286, in which Hugh is styled *clericus de consilio* (i.e. for *concilio*, a distinction not always made in the Middle Ages and certainly not at this period). That this means *the* Clerk of the Council, and not merely *a* clerk of the Council, is clear from the context, which is as follows:

> The keeper of the Wardrobe, Mr. William de Louth
> The Controller of the Wardrobe, Mr. William de March
> The Cofferer
> The Clerk of the Wardrobe

of Hereford, C.P.R. 88), in 1277 (Kirkstall Abbey, C.P.R. 208 for 1277), and in 1278 (See of Norwich, C. Cl. R. 501).

[1] C. Cl. R. 332, 543, 566; C.P.R. 297; and many other references in these volumes.
[2] C.P.R. (1280), 377.   [3] C.P.R. (1281), 454.
[4] Hamilton was deputy Chancellor in 1286–9 and Chancellor 1305–7.
[5] John Langton was Chancellor 1292–1302.
[6] *Cal. Chancery Warrants*, 7, 9–14, 19–22 (1282–4); C. Cl. R. (1283), 209.
[7] C. Cl. R. (July 1284), 271.

The Proctor at the Court of Rome
The Proctor *in partibus Francie*
The keeper of the household of the king's children
The buyer of the Wardrobe
Hugh de Kendale *clericus de consilio Regis*
Mr. Simon the king's surgeon
Two clerks, Walter de Dolve and John de Montibus [received robes in the next account. The reason is given as *de curialitate Regis*]
Two foreign merchants.[1]

The Controller of the Wardrobe held the Privy Seal, and was called from the time of Benstede (1295) *Secretarius Regis*.[2] Kendal was never styled this, and he was certainly neither Privy Seal nor Controller. Since he was obviously important and must have had a niche somewhere, I see him as just below Privy Seal in the Wardrobe, and just below the Vice-Chancellor in the Chancery. This conclusion is based on the available evidence. It seems incapable of conclusive proof at the moment, but it is not guesswork.[3]

As the steward's attorney when the steward was abroad, the Clerk would naturally conduct the foreign business of the Council, for this was part of the steward's function. It was noticed that in Henry III's reign, when it is possible to discover who the responsible clerk is, foreign affairs fell to the steward. So as a king's clerk (1280) and then (1281) the steward's attorney it seems that he must have been trained in foreign business.

It was the Secretary—at a later date Secretary of State for Foreign affairs—who dealt with the foreign correspondence or diplomatic relations, that is the Secretary or

[1] This is translated from a wardrobe account, in P.R.O. E. 101/351/17, of 18 Ed. I (1285). There are no other 'clerks of the council' in this list.

[2] *Handbook of British Chronology*, 89. John Mansel had been so described in the mid thirteenth century. As a diplomat and 'chief counsellor' (Matt. Par.) he was a great king's clerk.

[3] The first clerk of the council to be mentioned as such by James Baldwin in his *History of the King's Council*, pp. 362 f., is Gilbert de Roubiry (1290–5), who was Hugh de Kendal's successor. He became a judge in 1295 and d. 1320.

Clerk of the Council. The Secretary at this time prepared bills and letters to be sealed with the Signet. The Clerk was in some sort a Foreign Secretary, a chancery clerk, and later would be a Privy Councillor who kept the Signet.

If there was a Signet at this date Hugh probably kept it, in the Wardrobe, for he is listed among the Wardrobe staff, after the chief officials, and not with the other clerks of the Council. He died in 1297.[1]

Another such family, the Langfords of Hampshire, may also be taken as typical of the administrative and sociological history of the king's knights in the fourteenth century. Nicholas seems to have been the most important of them. He fought at Boroughbridge in 1322, where he was taken prisoner, and at the second Dunstable tournament in 1334.[2] About this time he acted as a commissioner of array for Derbyshire.[3] He had also been a knight of the shire for Derbyshire in January 1324. John de Langford, a knight in Hampshire in 1324, was also at Boroughbridge and his coat of arms indicates kinship.[4] He became Constable of Carisbrooke Castle, and Keeper of the Isle of Wight.[5] William de Langford was the member for Middlesex in 1344. He is described as 'chief servitor of the king's religion' in 1336, and Keeper of the New Temple, London, in 1333.[6]

In October 1331 Nicholas 'was and is' in the king's company, and so excused attendance at an eyre.[7] He had the bailiwick of the hundred of Tolmanslow or Tamslow, Derbyshire, for life in 1335.[8]

[1] *C. Cl. R.* (1297), 116.
[2] Boroughbridge roll No. 144, *paly of six or and gules, a bend argent* = Powell No. 469 (Nichol) = II Dunst. No. 52. (But No. 138 on the same Boroughbridge rolls gives Nicholas de Langeford *vert six lions rampant or.*) Cotgrave No. 492, Ashm. roll 15A No. 329, and Carlisle roll Nos. 130–2 have *baston* instead of *bend.* [3] *C. Cl. R.* (1333–7), 87, 95.
[4] John de Langford bore *paly of six argent and gules, on a chief azure a lion passant or* (Boroughbridge roll No. 112, cf. 144) = Powell 483.
[5] *C. Cl. R.* (1335–8), 435, 521.
[6] Ibid. 32, 308, 709. But query if this William is not a clerk?
[7] Ibid.. 348. [8] Ibid. (1337–9), 352.

It was not by the tenants-in-chief that the shire was run. Their influence decreased continually as the shire court fell more and more into the hands of the stewards and the squirearchy. After about 1300 the descent of the knights' fees has hardly more than an antiquarian interest, though of great value in helping to elucidate family history and the descent of manors. The seignorial administration of the shire is largely a matter of the separate administration of each manor by a resident tenant, and the public administration fell to these residents rather than to their overlords. For example, in 1295 the manor of Mapledurham Gurney passed from the main line of Bardolf of Wormegay in Norfolk to the younger sons. Sir John Bardolf, from about 1304, 'lived the life of an ordinary country gentleman of distinction'.[1] In 1311, as supervisor of array in Oxfordshire and Berkshire and leader of the levies there, he led his troops for the Scottish war at least as far as Roxburgh.[2] From the first, infantry levied by array were normally embodied by counties.

The continued importance in practice of the franchises is emphasized by the sheriff's inability to distrain Sir John Bardolf, as a knight of the shire, to provide sureties for his appearance at Westminster, because Mapledurham was within the Chiltern hundreds, and the lord of the honour of Wallingford had 'return of writs', so that the sheriff could not enter the liberty without a writ of *Non omittas propter libertatem*. Sir John attended Parliament nevertheless, being present at three sessions in 1313. In 1314 he was a justice of gaol delivery in Oxfordshire and Berkshire. In 1317 he was excused the office of coroner for Oxfordshire on the ground that he resided in Norfolk and Leicestershire for the greater part of the year. It may be suspected that this was an excuse, not a

[1] This paragraph owes much to A. H. Cooke, *The Early History of Mapledurham* (Oxon. Rec. Soc. iii (1925)), 20–1, 32.
[2] *Parl. Writs*, ii. 479. For the arms of Bardolf see Powell (G. 37), *azure three cinquefoils in pale or pierced of the field*. Cf. No. 77, the same *within a bordure engrailed argent*. The former is Bardolf of Wormegay in Norfolk.

reason, for Mapledurham might be thought to be a very desirable place to live in. The last and most distinguished of the Bardolfs to hold Mapledurham, though much at court under Edward III and Richard II, was a J.P. in 1386–93 and a commissioner of array.

Local Knights

It is absurd to suppose that these knights were unpaid servants of the community, yet this is often suggested. The spirit of devoted public service in the interest of the neighbours may have been strong in the Middle Ages, but there was always a *quid pro quo*, if not in the form of extortion or customary fees, as was general with unpaid local officials (sheriffs, coroners, verderers, etc.), then in the employment of king's knights or knights paid by the king as commissioners of array, constables of castles, escheators (though these were sometimes clerks), or keepers of vacant bishoprics, abbeys, and lay fiefs. Again, one may take a man like Ralph Bocking, who was steward of St. Edmondsbury when it was *not* vacant; for it was a royal abbey and the steward whether or not formally imposed by the king was very much a king's knight, and a Member of Parliament twenty-three times. These knights were of course paid a retaining fee and a salary as well by the king's household, and are to be found scattered about the few remaining wardrobe accounts. Sometimes this comes to light in the printed records, as with the Langford family, who may serve as a type for them all. Normally these men played along with the king or the magnates but on at least two occasions they intervened with decisive effect upon the course of events. The Bacheleria of 1259 is one instance: the Parliament of York (1322) perhaps another. The Good Parliament in 1376 is of course the most obvious of all.

Far from shunning elections, many knights were ineluctable in the pursuit of local office. Their efforts to

KNIGHTS IN THE FOURTEENTH CENTURY 49

become or remain verderers or coroners were blatant and unblushing. A brief glance at a few of them suggests the tag *capax imperii nisi imperasset*, and casts a gloomy and indirect light upon the workings of a shire court dominated by the stewards of magnates and a few other *buzones*. The number of verderers and coroners who have to be removed because incapacitated by 'old age and infirmity' or as being 'insufficiently qualified' (i.e. meaning usually, I suppose, having no lands in the county) is remarkable under Edward II. There is so much hankering after office by sick old men that we must believe any local office to have had considerable social value, or political use as a potential stepping-stone. To many people any taste of power acts like a drug. While the case of the Jorz family shows us that much of this jockeying for position was harmless, we also see that this family was on the fringe of a gang whose activities were much more sinister, for one of them rode with the Folevilles in the Robin Hood country, as verderer of Sherwood Forest.[1]

There were two men called Robert Jorz in this period. The first, who may have been the father, clung to office in a series of remarkable switches for eleven or more years. There is a writ of 1299 for the election of a verderer of Sherwood Forest in his place, as he has lately been elected a coroner for Nottinghamshire.[2] There is another writ ordering the election of a verderer to replace Jorz, this time because he is insufficiently qualified; this is dated 5 January 1309, so, unless he had sold his land, it had taken the county a decade to discover his disqualification. The point is, I believe, that this disqualification is (*temp.* Edward II) a frequent reason given for change of office. The shire court cannot possibly have been deceived

---

[1] The verderers are armigerous knights. Sir John Bevercotes (near Hoghton) was at Boroughbridge and is on Powell's roll. Thomas de Boulton (*vide* Chap. VI), who had been retaindered with Ralph Neville, became in 1328 a tax-collector in the East Riding of Yorkshire and a verderer, but was found to be insufficiently qualified (*C. Cl. R.* (1327–30), 207 and 35).

[2] *C. Cl. R.* (24 Sept. 1299). Cf. R. F. Hunnisett, *The Medieval Coroner*, 170.

about one of their own officials over such a period. There are three writs for the election of a coroner in his place: one is issued because he had just been elected verderer (again, presumably); another, dated 14 March 1315, as he was living too far from certain parts of the county; and the third, of 20 June 1316, because he was 'infirm'. All this is not to be taken too seriously. It sounds too similar to the old legal system of alternative defences that went on in civil cases until modern times. We are, I think, dealing with legal fictions and, though it is difficult to see the necessity for them in this and similar instances, the law makes a profit out of them, and the elusive petty criminal or 'wide boy' escapes.

This Robert knew the rules of the game. He had been an M.P. for Nottinghamshire in May 1306. Such men were in an excellent position to discuss aspects of local government with their fellow members, to explain that Robin Hood and his gang were a menace, and to understand the import of the Statute of Northampton, to which men like the second Robert Jorz gave their approval.

The second Sir Robert Jorz was M.P. for Nottinghamshire on five occasions between 1324 and 1340. It is a useful comment on the *Return of Members* that, though he is known to have been a knight, he is only so styled once out of five times.[1] In this too there is an atmosphere of evasion. He is identified on 22 July 1327 as Robert Jorz of Gedling, Nottinghamshire, and a member of the Foleville gang; and the record makes it clear that he is trying to slide out of some accusation.[2] While still coroner he was occupied, according to a cancelled writ of 11 August 1337,[3] with the affairs of certain magnates outside the county and with the king's business in Scotland. A writ of the same date emphasizes that it was indeed the

[1] Over a period of thirty years Alexander Neville was an M.P. and knight, but he is never styled knight in the *Return of Members* Jan. 1327–Apr. 1357. It is true that he was returned only seven times and there is a gap between 1337 and 1355. Perhaps he was at the wars.
[2] *C. Cl. R.* (1327), 213. [3] Ibid. 154.

king's business and that he was not engaged in the service of other lords.[1]

More serious offences, even homicide, were not unknown in the ranks of the Commons in this violent age. I do not know if more modern parliaments have been analysed as to their criminal content. Businessmen have on occasion to 'declare their interest', but, just as, according to the climber's maxim, 'crime ceases at 3,000 metres', so much is forgiven if a man can ascend to the plutocracy. For fourteenth-century Bedfordshire an analysis of M.P.s has been made by Miss Margery Fletcher and commented on by Professor Plucknett.[2] In a single decade (1327–36) five had been accused and four convicted of felonies.

These coroners were officers elected in the shire court to exercise and safeguard the rights of the Crown in certain criminal matters which might give rise to a prosecution for felony. His frequent post-mortems—when he decided the cause of sudden or violent deaths and recorded them on his rolls—have nothing to do with the inquests *post mortem* taken by the escheator on the death of a tenant-in-chief, and referred to in later times as the escheator's office. The coroner, usually but not always a knight, had also to deal with abjurations of the realm by convicted criminals, confessions of felons, and appeals of approvers. He had to organize outlawries promulgated in the county court, and in furtherance of these duties he had to 'attach or arrest witnesses, suspects, and others, appraising and safeguarding any lands and goods which might later be forfeited, recording all the details'.[3] He was at the height of his powers in the second half of the thirteenth century, but his position was considerably

[1] Ibid. 156.
[2] T. F. T. Plucknett on 'Parliament' in *The English Government at Work*, i (1327–36), 96 n. 1. Other county monographs are listed in the *Interim Report of the Committee on House of Commons Personnel and Politics* (Cmd. 4130, 1932).
[3] R. F. Hunnisett, *The Medieval Coroner* (C.U.P., 1961), 1. Mr. Hunnisett remarks (p. 5) that the law books give a greatly exaggerated picture, derived from the earlier rolls, of the coroner's powers.

weakened by the rise of keepers, later justices, of the peace. In social standing they were second in importance only to the sheriff, and, if not knights, had at least to be men of substance in their districts.

As with other responsible positions, some sought the office, and others evaded it by reason of age and infirmity,[1] or resigned after a short spell of duty, we know not why. It is doubtful whether the office of coroner was regarded as worth while for a first-class man, since he was unlikely in this period to achieve any higher professional status. Coroners had the usual opportunities for lining their pockets by petty extortion, but the world in which they moved was not usually that of bachelors and bannerets even if they themselves were knights. Their lives were sordid and reeked of the mortuary. They were on the same level as the verderers or minor forest officials, and often undertook this office either before or after being coroners.

The Jorz case is not cited by Mr. Hunnisett, but he gives a magnificent example in the writs replacing Thomas atte Bergh. The first four described him as insufficiently qualified, a fifth said that he was dead, and then two more were issued on the grounds of his insufficient qualification. In such cases, Mr. Hunnisett remarks, it is usually impossible to tell who provided the information, and whether the coroner was escaping from an unwanted office, or being forced from one he liked.[2] This must be true of many offices at all periods.

Composition of the Commons

Over a period of five hundred years many of the essential features in the composition of the Commons remained constant. It was possible to write in 1864:

It [the Lower House] consists of the heirs and younger sons of peers, of landed commoners and their relations, of moneyed men,

[1] R. F. Hunnisett, *The Medieval Coroner* (C.U.P., 1961), 1.
[2] Ibid. 183.

KNIGHTS IN THE FOURTEENTH CENTURY 53

of lawyers, merchants, and bankers, all as a rule investing in land as fast as their means and opportunities will allow. The members of the Lower House who do not come under these descriptions are few. It is, indeed, frequently said that the Lower House is elected so much by the influence of the Upper House, and the similar influence of large landed proprietors, as not to be sufficiently independent in its legislative functions.[1]

Writers on the fourteenth century have said much the same thing, but have more to say because of the increased scope in local government for the knights of the shire.

Many were, or had been, the retainers of magnates both ecclesiastical and lay; some were the sons of former members; many had trading interests; as the century progressed, an increasing number had been in the wars; probably the majority had served their counties in some other capacity, as sheriffs or coroners, as keepers or as justices of the peace, as tax-collectors, or commissioners of array. . . . It was by no means uncommon for a parliamentary knight to have been in the courts on a charge of felony; but they brought into parliament a wide range of administrative experience and knowledge of local conditions and, overlapping at one end with the bourgeoisie, their presence there prevented alignment into rigid social or professional groups and made possible their own consolidation with the burgesses into a single *collegium* or House of Commons.[2]

Professor Cam had already pointed out: The younger sons of Earls [and barons] become country gentlemen, the burgesses purchase land in the shire, the country gentlemen come into the boroughs.'[3] Or again, Professor

---

[1] *The Times* of 4 Feb. 1864. The knights are first recorded as sitting apart from lords and clergy in 1331. In 1323 they sat with citizens and burgesses in a separate place. It seems to be only after 1322 that the local gentry begin to infiltrate the towns, but this is hardly more than a personal impression, which began to crystalize when it was noticed that Simon de Foleville was elected for Nottingham. There are others this year.

[2] M. McKisack, *The Fourteenth Century* (Oxford, 1959), 1888–9. Wood-Legh, 'The Knights in Attendance in the Parliaments of Edward III', *E.H.R.* xlv (1932), 398–413, and 'Sheriffs, Lawyers, and Belted Knights in the Parliaments of Edward III', *E.H.R.* xliv (1931), 372–88.

[3] H. Cam, *Liberties and Communities*, 246.

McKisack says: 'The parliamentary knights included many old soldiers, men of wealth and standing in the shires with long experience of local government.'[1] It will be observed that none of these writers have observed the vital influence of king's knights as M.P.s. However, though incapable of proof, this may be thought just as significant as the influence allowed to Speakers under seignorial influence, which is now generally acknowledged.

Here we may add that there was uncertainty about the position of the sheriff, who in 1300 was to be elected by the shire. In 1311 this privilege was withdrawn by the Ordainers, but reintroduced in 1338 by Edward III, who finally provided in 1340 that they were to be in office for no more than a year and appointed by the Exchequer.[2] But the decline of the sheriff is not the decline of the county.[3] The knights and those of the gentry who were not knights but might have been[4] have always performed those tasks of local government which in the thirteenth and fourteenth centuries were gradually withdrawn from the sheriff and given to specialized officials. From 1330 Parliament, 'restored to its rightful dignity by the Statute of York [1322]', never meets without the Commons. The government had come to realize that as 'agents of propaganda and vehicles of public opinion' they were indispensable.[5] The bishops preached to them in 1327, whereas Edward I had hoped to obtain the same effect by public letters to the Pope and cardinals, nominally written by the barons but in reality the work of the royal wardrobe clerks, possibly the prothonotary, the result

---

[1] McKisack, op. cit., 393.
[2] Stubbs, *Const. Hist.*, Chap. XV, § 204.
[3] The sheriff remains the executive officer in the shire. 'He arrested suspects, carried out penalties adjudged by the courts, royal writs were addressed to him, prisoners entrusted to him. He held the shire and hundred courts, and collected the older sources of revenue.' In addition, other local officials worked through him so that his office was the centre of all the local government of the shire.
[4] See F. M. Powicke, *The Thirteenth Century*, 547.
[5] McKisack, op. cit., 104.

KNIGHTS IN THE FOURTEENTH CENTURY

then being circulated by a royal messenger to be sealed by as many barons as might be.[1] Edward III used declarations of his parliaments for similar propaganda against the French in 1335.

Edward, however, had no real affection for his knights and burgesses. The spirit of 1259 had died within him. When the knights and burgesses had made their money grant he sent them home, and got down to the business of governing the country from Westminster or wherever he happened to be.

If the deficiencies of the sheriffs' returns to the writs for the election of knights of the shire are made obvious by comparing the returns of different years one with another, they are immediately made more so by an examination of even one volume of the *Calendar of Close Rolls*. The volume for 1324–7 yields a total of ninety-one attendances of persons described as knights, but not so styled in the returns. On the same basis the whole run of sixteen volumes of the calendars for the period covered by this book might add 1,450 attendances of perhaps 300 knights (whom I have indexed), because if a man was returned once he was likely to be returned a number of times. A different picture is obtained from the collection of writs *de expensis* as entered on the close rolls. The point is of some importance, because it is not clear from the sheriffs' returns as printed whether the bulk of the members are knights or not, but it is obvious from the enrolments, even in the printed *Calendars of Close Rolls*, that the members returned are knights, unless otherwise styled in the returns, or unless another class of person is asked for in the writ to the sheriff. This has been tested in some hundreds of instances, through the writs *de expensis* of the first half of the fourteenth century.

[1] I have noted about a dozen such letters of the thirteenth and fourteenth centuries—most of them on church affairs.

The Parliament of Lincoln, 1327 (September)

There does not seem to have been a man-by-man inquiry into the status of the Commons since the *Return of M.P.s* (1878) and the *Calendars of Close Rolls* for the reigns of Edward II and Edward III were published, and for this reason, tedious and perhaps unnecessary though the task is, a new inquiry, particularly with regard to the seventy-four county members, should be undertaken.[1] A comparison of these two sources produces surprising results. The first parliament that can conveniently be tested is that of Lincoln (September 1327). If the close roll is to be believed only fifty knights came instead of seventy-four, so that, although the *Return* appears so defective when it indicates that no return was found for this or that county, it is as likely as not that no return was made, and that the parliaments of this period were much below strength in the number of knights present.

Yet a small mystery remains. Three men were returned to this parliament whose behaviour or fate is anomalous. Constantine de Mortimer was returned for Norfolk, but, while his companion John de Ormesby had his writ *de expensis*, Constantine did not. When he was again returned for the parliament at York on 2 February 1328 Constantine took his wages as did the others.[2] Of the two Staffordshire men returned, John de Swynnerton had his writ, but Philip de Somervill's name is not on the close roll. But he was a well-known Staffordshire man, M.P. at least six times between 1322 and 1336, and 'largely re-modelled Balliol'.[3] With these examples in mind, and there are

[1] *C. Cl. R.* Ed. III (1327–30), Preface dated 15 July 1896; (1330–3) 1898; and also to vol. xiv (1374–7), 1912. The text of these volumes, having been prepared by W. H. Stevenson, is excellent: the indexes are inadequate. In this close-roll list of knights at the parliament of Lincoln the persons returned are specifically referred to as 'Knights' in the heading of the entry.

[2] *C. Cl. R.* (1327–30), 374; *Return*, 81. The editors point out that Northumberland, though it returned members, had no writ *de expensis*, so they must have been aware of the oddities here noticed.

[3] McKisack, *The Fourteenth Century*, 507. Somervill had a wood in Cannock

KNIGHTS IN THE FOURTEENTH CENTURY

others,[1] there is less temptation to regard the omission of Thomas de Foxle for Berkshire as deliberate. He was returned again in 1332 and 1337 but in each case *loco militis*.[2] There is also a remarkable instance in the Parliament of Northampton of 1328, noted in the *Calendar of Close Rolls* (p. 388), where thirty boroughs that returned members are omitted from the lists of those receiving writs *de expensis*, but here the reluctance to serve seems to reappear like a ghost from some nineteenth-century textbook.

The returns sent in by the sheriff may not therefore be taken at their face value. When told to elect knights, the status of the persons elected is sometimes given and sometimes not. Even on the internal evidence of the writs themselves, there is no consistency. The man may be styled *miles* or *chivaler*: or he may in one year be so styled and in another not. Thirdly, he may be elected, as always in Oxfordshire,[3] *loco militis*, and fourthly he may be styled *armiger* or esquire, or even *vallettus*, i.e. yeoman or (at a certain period) franklin, like Chaucer's franklin; though the word, being English, naturally is not found in the returns. As a result of collecting the names and status of M.P.s from the returns, it is found that about 10 per cent more of the members were knights than would at first sight appear. By adding the evidence of other sources, such as the rolls of arms and other chancery enrolments, this percentage is greatly increased, and it is true that the majority at all times were belted knights.

Chase in Staffs. and land in Notts. (*C. Cl. R.* (1327), 231). He founded six theological fellowships at Balliol.

[1] Men returned for Derby. (2), Lincs. (2), Notts. (2, one for the sixth time), and Wilts. (Sir Edmund Gacelyn) had no writs. Surrey and Sussex sent excuses. For Devon, Dorset, Essex, Herts., Somerset, no returns were found.

[2] Thomas de Foxle is not indexed. John de Foxle, on the other hand, is in *C. Cl. R.* (1327), 31. He, too, was an M.P. well known in Berks. and Kent (*Parl. Writs*, 1324) and had been a Swan Knight in 1306.

[3] I do not know why Oxon. always sent men *in loco militis*. Rutland and Wiltshire regularly sent knights and always described them as such in the returns.

It remains true that many shire members were not knights, and that the number of actual knights varies quite widely from parliament to parliament. Also the number of persons returned many times is high. Multiple representation is frequent, especially in the West Country. This has already been commented on by Professor A. F. Pollard.[1] The practice varies from shire to shire. Personal idiosyncrasies of the sheriff's office perhaps played their part. If so, the answer not only will change from county to county, but may change every few years within the same county.

The number of knights returned as M.P.s tended to increase when Edward III was in power. Using only the returns themselves, plus the Boroughbridge Roll, we find in 1322 only twenty-eight who are known to have been knights. By using other sources we can arrive at a figure of thirty-eight, but only eight are described as knights in the returns. In this parliament at York (2 May) there were many very experienced members. There may have been 32 new members, though I doubt it, but certainly 19 were returned for the second time, 19 were serving for the third, 12 for the fourth, 3 for the sixth,[2] and 2 for the seventh time. Yet in 1324, when the country was at a low ebb, the writ for the first time contains the words 'two knights or others'.[3] In this year the word *chivaler* is first used. The deposition of Edward II seems not to have affected the composition of the commons. On the evidence of the returns, the rolls of arms, and the close rolls there are in the 1338 (July) parliament only ten men who should be styled knights, perhaps because so many active knights had been mustered for the war. In 1339 (14 January, 3 February) there were 20; in 1350, 8; in 1360, 12; in 1368, 13; in 1369, 33; in 1376 (the Good

---

[1] Pollard, *Evolution of Parliament* (1926), App. II, 411–14.
[2] *Ret.*, 71.
[3] Sir Richard de Perers, Kt., is returned for the sixth time for Herts. He had been in Lancaster's retinue at the first Dunstable tournament.

KNIGHTS IN THE FOURTEENTH CENTURY 59

Parliament), 40. Stubbs remarked that 'they were reduced to a dozen in 1377',[1] but this is not so. Even my incomplete analysis shows at least twenty-one. A close analysis, using all the available sources, would, I am sure, reveal a different state of affairs and a higher percentage of knights in every parliament tackled.

Re-election

Evidence for re-election of knights[2] later in the century is similar, and little purpose would be served by displaying it in full,[3] but a few examples may be listed. In the decade 1330–40 many of the members were very young, and they reappear twenty years later in the Black Prince's retinue; but still more already had twenty years of parliamentary experience:

Ralph de Bocking 22 times for Suffolk.

John Cokeyne 12 times for Derbyshire (between 1335 and 1362) but is never styled knight, though Powell's roll No. 96 gives arms for him.

Thomas Corbet was migratory. A Shropshire tenant, he was M.P. for Surrey in 1322–3.

Hugh de Croft, too, was a most discursive person. A Shropshire knight (P.R.A. 968) he was in the Earl of Arundel's retinue first Dunstable tournament (I Dunst. 156) and sat (or should it be stood?) for Herefordshire (1314), Huntingdonshire (1332), and Bedfordshire (1334).

Many such examples[4] could be given for every parliament of the century. The session that began on 14

[1] *Const. Hist.* iii, Chap. XXI, § 479, 567.
[2] The detailed study of this subject was initiated by Professor Gailland Lapsley in *E.H.R.* (1912), and Professor Sir Goronwy (at that time Mr. J. G.) Edwards in 1918 in 'The Personnel of the Commons in the Reign of Edward II', in the Tout *festschrift*.
[3] For the second half of the century, and more particularly from the reign of Richard II and through the fifteenth century, the question has been well resolved by K. B. McFarlane in 'Parliament and Bastard Feudalism', *T.R.H.S.* (1944), 53–73.
[4] See also T. F. T. Plucknett in *The English Government at Work, 1327–36*,

November 1322 is the first to which six *valetti* or yeoman or franklins were returned—for Herefordshire, Leicestershire, and London and Middlesex. In the same year one Ralph de Beauchamp (the name speaks for itself) was a Winchester burgess, and at different times Sir John Morys or Moriz was M.P. for the borough and shire of Cambridge.[1]

Most M.P.s in the fourteenth century had land in two or three or even more counties. It is hard to see what determined a prospective candidate's choice of county, if by reason of his qualifications he had a choice. Cases are heard of men elected against their will, but these are very rare: most people at any rate would be willing to serve if it did not cost them more than they could afford, and medieval M.P.s received the current 'rate for the job' without dispute.

Do they indeed make their own choice or are they foisted upon the shire court by a great magnate? The mere fact that they perambulated from county to county disposes of the idea that such men had any reluctance to serve. Westminster was as attractive to ambitious men in the fourteenth century as it is today. Yet there can be no doubt that many candidates were told by their lords where to go and what to do. In other words the knights and the burgesses from towns under seignorial influence were not independent of the lords. A knight in retainder to the Duke of Lancaster could hardly take the lead against him without losing his position in the Duke's retinue.

There are many anomalies. Why is one of the Corbets, a Shropshire family, a member for Gloucester in 1318? Or why do the four knights of the Gascelyn family fluctuate between Wiltshire and Gloucestershire?[2]

for an analysis of the careers of Bedfordshire knights from Miss M. Fletcher's London M.A. thesis 1933. Other county monographs are listed in the *Interim Report of the Committee on House of Commons Personnel and Politics* (Cmd. 4130, 1932), 12–13.

[1] See *D.N.B.* xiii. 1068–9; Sir John *flor.* between 1330 and 1340.

[2] His arms are in the P.R.A. and the first Dunstable roll (de la Commure).

An early example of rigging the election of an M.P. comes from Lancashire in 1329–30, before even the Statute of York had made the knights of the shire an essential constituent of Parliament. The interest of this election is twofold. There is the negative aspect of a county court that is not interested in what its representatives did at Westminster, showing clearly that they sent representatives only because they had been ordered so to do and not because they wished to make their own views known in Parliament. Their only interest in the matter, as appears from a detailed account of the sheriff's ill deeds,[1] was that, if they had elected their own men instead of having the sheriff's nominees foisted upon them, the expenses would have been very much less.[2] It is not explained how this would have come about, but it seems reasonably clear that they would have chosen a yeoman or franklin instead of a knight, at half the expense unless the latter was a banneret. This might have happened at that date in any shire court, for they were declining, run by the magnates and the sheriff.

There is nothing particularly significant in all this. Thirteenth- and fourteenth-century officials of all kinds were in the habit of lining their pockets by petty extortion.[3] It is so common that it is difficult to decide where 'tipping' for services rendered leaves off and payment for protection or acquiescence in crime begins. There is nothing about the return of an M.P. to distinguish it, if we take the sheriff's point of view, from the election of any other local official such as a coroner or a verderer. As soon as someone sees the possibility of turning a quick penny, corruption is likely to appear, and in parliamentary elec-

[1] H. Tupling, *South Lancashire in the Reign of Edward II* (Chetham Soc., 1949).
[2] Professor H. Cam, *Liberties and Communities*, 246, takes another view. She suggests that the difference between paying 2*s*. a day for a franklin or yeoman (*valettus*) or 4*s*. for a knight 'was not of overmastering importance to the shire community'.
[3] Denholm-Young, *Seignorial Administration* (1937), 109–19.

tions it was to continue in one form or another until the age of the Ballot Act.

The last example was taken from the inquiry into misgovernment in South Lancashire in and after 1322. We cannot generalize confidently for the rest of England until far more plea rolls have been published, but much of the sporadic rioting, looting, pillaging, and feuding with neighbours that went on is reflected in the close rolls of the Chancery.

There was further corruption in 1319 and 1320 when William le Gentil, sheriff of Lancashire, returned as M.P.s persons who had not been chosen by the shire, and these persons procured writs for expenses on which they claimed twice the amount that properly elected M.P.s would have done.[1] I take this to mean that Earl Thomas of Lancaster did not care, or was unable to control the sheriff. However, the sheriff was not at that time the Earl's legal nominee, so perhaps the Earl is blameless.

The payment of members is in one way puzzling, because, as Professor Helen Cam, has remarked, it was cheaper to send a franklin (like Chaucer), i.e. a *valettus* or yeoman as the central government would have said, at 2s. a day, instead of a knight at 4s. The rate was fixed, after fluctuations, in 1327.[2]

But 4s. a day was the pay since Edward I's reign of a knight banneret, not a knight bachelor. The bannerets were few, and when they appear in Parliament do not sit as representatives but are summoned individually as magnates. However, the representatives were paid for the duration of Parliament plus travelling-time there and back—eight days for Cornwall or Cumberland, though the latter was by far the more difficult and dangerous journey; one day from Oxford or Cambridge. The burden of payment fell on the shire, and was met in Leicestershire in 1300 by a rate of 4d. on every carucate, but was more usually assessed by hundreds and vills and

[1] Tupling, op. cit., 119. [2] Cam, op. cit., 238–9.

KNIGHTS IN THE FOURTEENTH CENTURY 63

collected by hundred bailiffs. If you became an M.P. or a local official (nominally unpaid) or were impressed into the army it was, in the thirteenth and fourteenth centuries, the neighbours who had to pay.[1]

The Commons in Parliament

The growth of the Commons after the Statute of York in 1322 is rapid. Their part in the deposition of Edward II was played not in Parliament alone. Mr. C. Martin has remarked that Sir William Trussel, Kt., a royal official (in anticipation of 1376) who presided at the tribunal which passed sentence of death on Hugh de Spenser the younger at Hereford on 24 November 1326, and also in January at Kenilworth,[2] 'voiced to Edward II the whole nation's renunciation of him'. As a Northamptonshire knight he bore *argent frette de goules besaunte de or*.[3] Knights of this name were respectively justice in eyre in Bedfordshire in 1254[4] and sheriff of Kent in 1296–8.[5]

[1] Before the rate was fixed, Surrey paid in 1324 at 3s. 4d. a day, two days travelling to the parliament, 24 days there, and two days returning—a total of £9. 6s. 8d. for the two knights. Cornwall paid less: the two county members received a total of £8. 15s. for 35 days (a week there and a week back) at 2s. 6d. a day (*C. Cl. R.* (1324), 160). Sending men from Cornwall to Carlisle or York (e.g. 1318 and 1322) or from Northumberland to Westminster was obviously twice as expensive, and the banneret's rate of pay adopted in 1327 would cost the shire £6 a month, or in modern terms £600 a month, not £600 a year, as it was until recently. There is a collection of writs *de expensis* giving details shire by shire in *C. Cl. R.* (1327), 107, 225. The routes taken by a few horsemen travelling together need further study. It could be done roughly by making a royal itinerary and comparing it with the roads as marked in Patterson's *Roads*, as the main lines of travel were the same until the nineteenth century.

[2] 'Walter Burley', *Oxford Studies Presented to Daniel Callus* (O.H.S., N.S. xvi, 1964), 194–230, especially 215 f. Because he was steward of the Leicester honour in Northants. and escheator South of Trent (1311–32), *C.P.R.* (1327–30) contains many references to one or more than one William Trussel. The equation on p. 125 is based on the *Historie Dunelm. Scriptores Tres*, Surtees Soc. (1829), 127.

[3] P.R.S. 780 = Collins 247.

[4] *Ann. Dunst.* 192 (1254), and cf. Collins's roll 247, 416, where 247 = P.R.S. 780, and 416 is a fifteenth-century addition having *Or* for *Azure*.

[5] Sir William Trussel, the escheator of 1311–12, and his son, who played an equally important role in 1343, are conflated in *C. Cl. R.* Both were Lancastrians

Work of the Knights in Parliament

The reign of Edward I is the last period of successful direct rule by the king and his ministers. There comes a 'gradual movement of the law-courts away from the legislature. . . . When the law-maker is his own interpreter (as in the period ending with the death of Hengham on 18 May 1311) the problem of a technique of interpretation does not arise.'[1] Professor Plucknett is here stating that when Edward I and his judges were all dead the interpretation of the laws made by them had to be left to the courts. It may be suggested that lawyers realized this when they fixed the date between the *Vetera Statuta* and the *Statuta Nova* at 1327, but this raises a large issue with which Plucknett was not in that context concerned—not only the nature of the legislating body, but the way in which statutes were created, by petition from below instead of ordinance from above.[2]

The relations of town and countryside are not a matter that concerns us in itself: what matters here is the relation of local knights to neighbouring burgesses. This is particularly close in the south-west. Local representation, whether of town or county is very much a family affair. This is not a corruption and the boroughs were not rotten. It was so in Wales, and must be accepted as part of the old British or Celtic way of life, where ties of blood most strictly regulated all their dealings. Cornwall, Devon, Dorset, and Somerset were each for natural reasons royalist and conservative and included five such boroughs in each

and the father is No. 41 on the Boroughbridge roll. Though in the older literature, including an excellent article in *D.N.B.* by W. E. Rhodes, the confusion is pointed out, the matter has not been clarified. See A. F. Pollard, *Evolution of Parliament*, 126, for the Speaker of 1343.

[1] T. F. T. Plucknett, *Statutes and their Interpretation in the Fourteenth Century*, 164–5.

[2] These petitions to the king in parliament, or in council, have provoked a number of important articles. See the *Handbook of British Chronology* (1961), 494–5.

KNIGHTS IN THE FOURTEENTH CENTURY 65

shire; there were three in Wiltshire and eight in the south-east. In the north, apart from the county towns and Hull and Scarborough, such towns did not exist.

Elsewhere the relation is still close. There is no sharp line between county families and burgesses. In Staffordshire a Trumwyme is a burgess in 1327 and one had been a knight of the shire before that. Sir John de Longuevill sat for Huntingdonshire, and in 1328 for the borough of Northampton. He had been a Swan Knight (1306) and is in the P.R.A. He has been identified as a justice of assize, *oyer et terminer*, and gaol delivery *temp.* Edward I and Edward II. He is likely to be the man who would have restricted the power of the king by arguing, in a famous gloss on Bracton, that he who has a *comes* has a *socius* and therefore a master.[1] Northampton was much on the baronial side, and they came near to having a university there. In Lancashire, about the same time, Gilbert (1320–1), William (1323), and Henry de Haydok (1329, 1330) are knights of the shire, but in 1332 Henry de Haydok (1320) is a burgess. In 1332 and 1336 John de Secheville, who came from what had originally been a Kent county family, was burgess for Tavistock. Thomas de la Rokele and John de Grey (whose names are sufficient to reveal their social status) sat for Norwich.

In this period, then, knights kept cropping up in boroughs or shire courts alternately as if they had little preference. In the case of double counties it could happen that the same man was chosen for both. Yet it was not always two counties under one sheriff that suffered this indignity (or embraced this economy?). John le Mareschal served Hertfordshire and Buckinghamshire in 1328–9. Dorset and Devon each elected Humphrey de Beauchamp in 1313. John de la Poile was similarly elected in September 1313 for Middlesex and Surrey, and in September 1314 Richard de Rivers was returned for Berkshire,

---

[1] *Select Passages from Bracton and Azo* (Selden Soc.), 125. Also in Lodge and Thornton, *Documents*, 10.

Essex, and Gloucestershire. Robert de Stanegrave was chosen member for Surrey and Kent in 1328.[1]

They were migratory, these fourteenth-century local knights. Robert Burdet sat sometimes for Warwickshire, sometimes for Leicestershire. John de la Haye moved from Cambridge to Hertfordshire, and then Buckinghamshire. Sir John le Rous had represented four different shires by 1336.

There seems to be a tendency for some honest folk to stick to their own counties, while the professional busybodies hasten from one side of the realm to the other in search of a seat.[2] There also continues to be in the decade 1330–40 a hard core of old parliamentary hands, not belted knights, but country squires who are re-elected time after time for the same constituency. The practice has grown up, and is now firmly established, of electing persons for counties with which they have no family territorial links, because many of them are in retinue and receive from the great man who contracts with them a grant of lands or a rent-charge on lands on his fee. This must gradually but inevitably change the pattern of feudal holdings, so that the form of a knight's name in many instances gives no clue to where he lives, and an M.P. for X does not have to reside there, but simply to have property there. Apart from being retaindered in counties other than their place of residence, most substantial knights had lands in more than one county.

For the second half of the century and later—and especially the parliaments of Richard II—the status, circumstances, and careers of M.P.s have been fully investigated. The features already noted constantly recur,

[1] Professor Cam has noted other examples: William of Goldington for Appleby in 1302 and 1305 and Westmorland in 1307. Matthew of Crawthorne for Exeter 1318–22 and Devon in 1328.

[2] And even in 1337 (see under Wake, the north-country family, a member for London and Middx.: there is another example in the same parliament) from one *end* of the realm to the other. Richard de Morby was M.P. for Oxon. in 1330, but Yorks. in 1322.

so it will be sufficient to take as an uninvolved but typical family the Bonevilles of Shute in Somerset. Nicholas Boneville of Shute and Devon is No. 45 on the Boroughbridge roll of arms (1322), and occurs again on Powell's roll as No. 203 (*c.* 1350). In 1324 he was returned as a knight for Devon. He was a very experienced county member, but has not been found as a king's knight or royal official. The family was a rising one at this date: they do not seem to be found in thirteenth-century lists of knights, but they were fully eligible for Parliament from the time of Edward I. It was under Edward III, from 1366, that they became M.P.s for Somerset, Sir William Bonville having been returned nineteen times.[1] Re-election of this type, and most of the other features mentioned, is a constant factor in medieval parliaments from 1275 to 1485.

The relation of the Commons to the Lords was governed in the last resort by the personal tie between so many of them, the facts of retainder, but on some matters they had divergent interests. The magnates already controlled, or could if they wished control, many county courts, and thus the return of candidates to their liking. From 1307 to 1360 they tried to extend and consolidate this aspect of their power by insisting on great men as keepers of the peace and local justices. The local knights wanted judicial powers in addition to the police duties of inquiry and arrest that they had always, or at any rate since 1194, possessed. They were in a position to make their views known effectively because as sheriffs there were seven to ten of them in every parliament between 1328 and 1336.[2] Also, though the position of Parliament as the concentration of the local courts is often a matter

[1] The Bonville arms were *or on a bend sable three mullets argent*. For many later instances see K. B. McFarlane, 'Parliament and Bastard Feudalism', *T.R.H.S.* (1944), 53-73.

[2] Wood-Legh, *E.H.R.* (1931), 373. This article was cited by Professor H. Cam, 'The Legislators of Medieval England' (Raleigh Lecture, 1945), *Proc. Brit. Acad.* xxxi, 132-58.

for comment, it is not always realized that, by the time this had become a fact, the local courts had fallen into the hands of the *Buzones*, many of whom were the stewards of great men. On this topic it is nowadays almost obligatory to cite as an instance Peter de la Mare, Speaker of the Good Parliament in 1376 and sometime steward of the Earl of March,[1] and then to discuss Sir Thomas Hungerford, steward to the Black Prince and John of Gaunt, and Speaker in 1377 owing to Gaunt's influence. Before he died in 1398 he had been M.P. for Wiltshire eleven times and for Somerset four times, having been returned for both counties in 1389–90.[2] Other members of the family were M.P.s in the fourteenth century—Robert sat five times for Wiltshire (between 1316 and 1339), while John was returned for both Lyme Regis and Melcombe Regis in May 1335. In the fifteenth century the family proliferated in Oxfordshire and Gloucestershire as well as Wiltshire. The Speaker's son by his second wife was Walter, Lord Hungerford (d. 1449). There are many such county families in England and Scotland which have a far longer record of stability and public service than that of most of the peerage.

The history of these two Speakers illustrates the general theory that the Commons were territorially or feudally, or as bastard feudatories, dependent on the Lords, but this did not entail complete loss of independence when it came to taxation or policy-making.

This same territorial and feudal dependence is evident throughout the history of Parliament until the nineteenth century; but the behaviour of the dependent knights in 1258, 1322, and 1376 leaves no doubt that the *Bacheleria*

[1] Peter de la Mare, the Speaker without title in 1376.
[2] He married a neighbour, Eleanor, daughter and heiress of Sir John Strug of Heytesbury, and secondly Joan, heiress of Sir Edmund Hussey of Holbrook. There is a good account of him and his relatives in *D.N.B.* x. In 1369 he bought from Lord Burghersh the manor of Farleigh Montfort, since called Farleigh Hungerford, the chief residence of his descendants. He had licence to crenellate it in 1383. He died 3 Dec. 1398 at Farleigh.

needed only a leader to assert themselves as a class with interests often opposed to those of the magnates. There was, indeed, a stopping-point at which they screwed up their courage, and then told the lords what must be done. This was made much easier by the device of intercommuning.[1] As territorial dependants they could be complaisant in many matters (cf. the J.P. system), but, when their own interests coincided with those of their country, they could, even at this period in the Middle Ages, 'speak for England'. Their Speaker spoke for the Commons and not for their territorial lords. The flare-up came when the Speaker of the Commons was also the representative of a powerful baronial section that was in opposition to the government. In 1322 it had been, as much as anything, the support of the great civil servants that mattered.

Influence of Kings and Lords on the House of Commons

As usual in English history before the reform bills, the Lords or the government had by the fourteenth century the means of dominating the Commons. Some examples in the later part of the century are nowadays common knowledge. It was in the nature of society that it would take much provocation so to rouse the knights that they would act independently or even in opposition to the lords. Not so the burgesses. Edward III in the first half of his reign often hoped to drive a better bargain by negotiating with the merchant as a separate estate, as upon occasions his grandfather had done. It was not only the lords but the king who had a stake in the behaviour of the Commons. Apart from boroughs on Crown land, especially in the south-west, and certain shires that for one reason or another were normally royalists, the king could

[1] J. G. Edwards, *The Commons in Medieval English Parliaments* (London, 1958).

expect the election of a number of experienced officials (as could the magnates) already in his service. The most obvious examples of magnate influence are found in the fourteenth-century Speakers who were at the same time baronial or seignorial stewards. Precisely the same line of thought shows that we should have expected to find the king's stewards active in the House of Commons. They are indeed there and the parallel is exact, but not so obvious, because the reference is to the king's escheators, who for a brief period were styled his stewards, and to men who did the work of stewards, though they were not so styled, such as keepers of the temporalities of great religious houses or of bishoprics. So the really professional M.P.s turn out to be king's knights, that is household knights, though this is concealed for us, as Hungerford and Peter de la Mare were for long concealed, because the style king's knight is rarely found in the published records of the fourteenth century. They were men, together with the king's bannerets, of the first importance as administrators in peace and as staff officers in war, but, perhaps because they were so well known, their status is not given once in a hundred times in any of the printed calendars or chronicles of the period. We may read volume after volume of chancery enrolments without discovering who these men were. It is easier, working from printed sources, to make a list of Lancastrian bannerets, or bannerets of the Black Prince, than it is to list even the more important knights of the royal household. Thus it is noted that Sir Ralph de Bocking, Kt., was elected for Suffolk twenty-three times and returned twenty-two times, but he is never styled knight, or king's knight, in the years 1325–40, 1343, or 1357. Yet when his career is examined in detail he is found to be just that—a member of the king's household with a retaining fee and summer and winter robes, one of the keepers of the temporalities of the Abbey of Bury St. Edmunds during the vacancy of 1327, and a royal commissioner on numerous other occasions. So circumstances worked for the government in 1377 because the Speaker was in league with John of Gaunt, earlier the Black Prince's party, and perhaps took the Commons with him. It seems to me that it was this parliament that was normal, and the Good Parliament that was packed, not vice versa. The Good Parliament was a natural phenomenon like the *Bacheleria* of 1258, and on each occasion there was found a natural leader—the Lord Edward or Peter de la Mare. Any packing was due to the natural instincts of the electorate. Further action was unnecessary. The opposition to the government found an outlet through the Earl of March (Edmund Mortimer), and, as in 1297, the Earl Marshal was demoted.

In a sense the House of Commons in the fourteenth century was always packed, because the king had his household knights elected when he could, and the great lords sent their stewards and household knights to those shire courts which were under their influence. Thus the history of the House of Commons conforms to the pattern of English administrative development, and in this the lords were merely (as in estate management in general) following the king's example. For the king was not backward in helping to people the Commons with his household knights. They may be expected in counties where the royal demesne was extensive and made it possible for the king to control the shire court. For example Thomas de Lucy on 23 September 1336 was elected for Cambridgeshire. He had been knighted at the king's order on or before 23 July 1333.[1] He had been at the second Dunstable tournament in 1334. William de Lucy, who had been a Swan Knight (No. 209) in 1306, became M.P. for Warwickshire in 1312, 1322, 1324, and 1328.

A good example of fourteenth-century practice is found in the history of the Maltravers or Mautravers family, the father being in the Lords, while the son and one or more

[1] *C. Cl. R.* (1334), 226.

cousins were in the Commons. Whoever was M.P. or were M.P.s a number of them were king's knights and bannerets and held numerous public offices.[1]

Historians sometimes speak of M.P.s as if they entered Parliament as the climax of a career of public service, civil or military. It is true to say rather that for an ambitious man it was an opportunity to enlarge his career *pari passu* with other activities. For the ancient warriors and retired civil servants we look, then as now, to the Lords rather than to the Commons—among the bishops and bannerets who received their individual writs of summons.[2]

[1] See *D.N.B.*, s.v. Maltravers; where C. L. Kingsford elucidates this pedigree, and *G.E.C.*, s.v. Mautravers, 578–85. John Maltravers (d. 1297), of Lytchett Maltravers in Dorset, had a son Sir John (1266–1343) and a grandson Baron John (1290?–1365), who as a young man in 1318 was M.P. for Dorset, and later keeper, with Thomas Gurney, of the deposed Edward II at Berkeley Castle. He became Steward of the Royal Household in 1330 and was summoned to Parliament as a baron in that year. On the fall of Isabella and Mortimer he fled to Germany and lived there and elsewhere for many years until Edward III restored him (1345–52).

[2] In the Lords, a few men like Chandos. But this book is dealing primarily with the country gentry, and the bannerets by this time had grown beyond the status of mere gentry. So this note is confined to 'simple knights' (*milites simplices*). Sir Robert de Bikenor, M.P. for Wiltshire in 1334 and 1336, was an escheator in the south-west and the Queen's steward in Devon and Cornwall. Otto de Bodrigan, a Cornish knight in the 1324 *Parl. Writs.* list, went on a pilgrimage, which was extremely fashionable in the period between the loss of the Holy Land and the outbreak of the Hundred Years War, to St. James, Compostella, in 1323–4, and in the same year was M.P. for Cornwall. He was Keeper of Lundy Island, under the sheriff of Devon, but rebelled with Thomas of Lancaster and was fined 1,000 marks in 1327. By 1329 he had been forgiven, and was once more in favour (*C. Cl. R.* (1327–30), 20, 30, 60, 199, 503). The family arms are on the Galloway roll of 1300, No. 227, for Henry de Bodrigan. For the pedigree see my book on the Rolls of Arms of 1334–5 (forthcoming).

III

THE LOVETOT-LANGTON SCANDAL

LESSER folk are often hurt when great men are at odds. So it was with Sir John Lovetot when he was embroiled with Edward I's war and finance minister Walter Langton in a quarrel probably engineered by the implacable Archbishop Winchelsey, who lived long enough to give a lead to Edward II's 'political bishops'. Sir John was one of three king's bannerets, members of the royal household, who turned traitor and suffered for their treason. It was characteristic of medieval *causes célèbres* that charges of witchcraft, sorcery, and intercourse with the devil should be brought as they had been against Hubert de Burgh in the 1230s. The case of Simon Fraser, a Scot, was one of straightforward treachery, and though he had fought for the king at Falkirk and Caerlaverock his head was placed on London Bridge with a fanfare of trumpets.[1] But Lovetot, who, unlike the others, had committed neither fraud nor treason, died obscurely. The Lovetots were people of good standing in Yorkshire.[2] John, the judge, died in 1294 leaving a widow Joan de Briançon, the stepmother of the plaintiff, who complained

---

[1] *Ann. Lond.* 148. See further *History and Heraldry*, 34 and n. 2.

[2] The Lovetot family had held an eleventh-century barony in Hallamshire (*Early Yorkshire Charters*, iii, ed. William Farrer, 3; and vi, ed. C. T. (now Sir Charles) Clay, 209) which descended in the thirteenth century to the Furnivalls of Nottingham, who also obtained the Huntingdonshire barony (Dugdale, *Bar.*). The elder Lovetot, a judge, bought up property in Essex field by field round his estate, and at Bures in Suffolk. The barony consisted of ten fees with Sutho in Hunts. as its *caput* (*Cal. I.P.M.* III, No. 207, and *C. Cl. R.* (1296–1302), 415, Joan Lovetot's dower). This Lovetot was a member with Anthony Bek, John de Vescy, and Mr. Thomas de Suddington or Sodington (a lawyer and private consultant) of an embassy to the Duke of Brabant on 20 June 1284 (*Foed.* I. ii. 643).

in 1302 that Walter Langton, two years before his meteoric rise to fame, had committed adultery with Joan and had, with her assistance, strangled her husband in bed.[1] He also accused Langton of black magic.[2] This trumped-up business was facilitated by Langton's unpopularity with the baronage, whom he fell upon heavily about this time for deserting the army in Scotland and going abroad to tourney. Lovetot appears as a catspaw of those who opposed the king in 1297 over foreign service and other matters. Nothing is known against him, except his folly in causing Langton to be summoned to Rome, where he was put to great trouble and expense. Lovetot was eventually imprisoned in Newgate, whence he was dragged in 1305, after the supposed settlement with Scotland, on a charge of homicide. He claimed his clergy on the ground that he had been a deacon two years before he was married. So he was handed over to the bishop and died mysteriously after five days in prison.[3]

The third king's knight who turned traitor was Sir Thomas Turberville, whose activities as a spy have been described by Sir Goronwy Edwards.[4] A little more has since come to light about him and his family. He was Sir Thomas Turberville of Crickhowell in Brecon,[5] as is shown by the heraldic evidence, for Hugh Turberville bears as arms a red lion rampant on a silver shield, and

[1] John Lovetot's arms were *argent a lion rampant, per fess gules and sable*, to which his son added 'a gold fleur-de-lis on the shoulder' of the lion as a mark of difference (Collins's roll Nos. 249, 486).

[2] Bliss, *Cal. Papal Letters*, 607. Thomas de Abberbury, Langton's agent and Lovetot's landlord, could have been the source of this information. See *The 'Liber Epistolaris' of Richard de Bury*, Index.

[3] *Flores Hist.* (Merton MS.), iii. 306. *Ann. Lond.* 137, suggests that he was hanged.

[4] J. G. Edwards, 'The Treason of Thomas Turberville', *Studies in Medieval History presented to Frederick Maurice Powicke* (Oxford, 1948), 296–309.

[5] *Dictionary of Welsh Biography* (English edn., 1959), says of Thomas: 'it is not clear that he belongs to the Crickhowel family. As in Glamorgan, the name Turberville persisted in cadet branches in Brecknock until the eighteenth century.' Of Hugh the *Dictionary* states that he had 8 lances and 6,000 marcher infantry under his command in 1283 and that he was 'deputy-constable' in 1284.

THE LOVETOT–LANGTON SCANDAL 75

Thomas, as his son, bears the same arms with a blue label.[1] Hugh, the father, was a king's banneret in 1285, 1286, and 1290. He was seneschal of Gascony in 1272 and died in 1293 before he could know of his son's treachery. In the same wardrobe accounts of 1285, 1286, and 1290, Thomas is found as a king's knight. His treason took place when he was captured by the French at Rioms in Gascony on 7 April 1295, by which time he was a banneret.[2] Four months later he returned to London as a spy, having agreed to work for the French while a prisoner in Paris. Nothing is known of his early life, nor at what age he left South Wales.

The poem of Turberville's treachery has here an especial interest on account of the context in which it is found, for it is one of the three constituents of Cott. MS. Caligula A. xviii, the other two being the Parliamentary Roll of Arms and the song of Caerlaverock. They are all of the same generation, and the manuscript itself is of North Country provenance. There is a possibility (no more) that the owner was Sir Robert Clifford of Clifford Castle in Herefordshire, who was thus a neighbour of the Turbervilles of Brecknock,[3] though about five or ten years junior to Sir Thomas Turberville. Clifford is prominent in the Caerlaverock Roll and became castellan of the castle when it was captured in 1300, and the P.R.A. is thought to have been begun when he was acting Marshal of England. Clifford may or may not have known his older and (until 1295) his more socially successful neighbour, for their marcher estates were fifteen or twenty miles apart, but the Turbervilles, father and son, and the Dorset branch

---

[1] Hugh is on Collins's roll No. 122, which is as Dering No. 156. Thomas is Collins's No. 373. The label would normally be removed on Hugh's death in 1293, but Collins's roll, thought to have been made in 1296, retains many outdated coats.

[2] Hem. (old edn.) 51–2; *Flores Hist.* iii. 92. A total of 13 knights and some 30 esquires were taken prisoner and sent to Paris.

[3] Clifford was under contract to the king on the Scottish border from 1295. He was born 1273 and killed at Bannockburn in 1314.

of the family,[1] as well as the Cliffords, were on Edward I's general staff.

The Boroughbridge Roll

This roll commemorates the royalist victory on 16 March 1322 over the troops of Thomas, Earl of Lancaster, at Boroughbridge in Yorkshire,[2] but is itself a list, though quite incomplete, of Contrariants: the king's forces are not mentioned at all.[3] The battle itself was almost bloodless, though its sequel was not, for the Earl's troops were taken by surprise and prisoners were numerous. Among the Lancastrian bachelors taken (as No. 54 on the list) was a herald king, Le Roi Bruiant. Prisoners were normally sent to royal castles for safe custody, so it is possible, perhaps even probable, that this Bruiant's roll was made in Northampton Castle, where the sheriff's records would be kept.[4] A Lancastrian herald would

[1] The Dorset Turbervilles held in Bere and Melcombe, and will be remembered by readers of Thomas Hardy's *Tess of the D'Urbervilles*. Henry de Turberville (or Trubleville), who was against the king in the young Marshal's rebellion of 1233, also became seneschal of Gascony. He went on an Italian expedition and died in 1239. The Turbervilles of Coty in Glamorgan, prominent on the Earl of Gloucester's fee (*C. Cl. R.* (1327), 11) were in 1327 Gilbert, a descendant of Richard, and William.

[2] Brit. Mus. Egerton MS. Add. 2850 (Cat. of Add. MSS. 1900–3, p. 391). A contemporary roll neatly written in the court hand of the period; it is 7″ wide and 9′ 7″ long and is made up of royal writs and the like, received by the sheriff of Northamptonshire, relating to the rebellion and the trial of Thomas Earl of Lancaster on 22 Mar. 1322, with other matter connected with the battle of Boroughbridge, hence printed in *Parl. Writs*, II. ii. 196. On the dorse are (i) the heraldic roll of 214 names and blazoned shields: this part is much darkened and in parts is not easily legible; (ii) magnates killed, bannerets taken prisoner there and elsewhere, bachelors taken prisoner, and, in another hand, whether they were hanged, surrendered, or fled overseas. The roll was edited by James Greenstreet in *The Genealogist*, N.S., vols. i (1884) and ii (1885) ;and see vol. xxi for an article on the battle by the Rt. Hon. Vicary Gibbs.

[3] Thirty-four men at least on the roll can be identified as prisoners, men hanged after the battle, or who fled overseas, or were pardoned and fined. Mr. Vicary Gibbs found 15 'Royalists', but evidence adduced from their later career is no proof of their loyalty in 1322.

[4] The castle of Northampton went with the county in the thirteenth and fourteenth centuries. Bruiant as a foreign herald could be excused for oddities of

naturally begin with a list, though a confused one, of his master's knights. His identity will be the subject of comment below.

At the battle Sir Andrew Harclay defeated and captured Lancaster, and had his own brief hour of triumph as Earl of Carlisle. It was just a year later that he intrigued with the Scots, as Lancaster had done, and was hanged for treason. In the course of the battle, a confused one because there was no time to draw up the combatants in proper formation—as reflected in the 'jumbled' state of the roll—the Earl of Hereford and four other barons were slain. Lancaster was tried and beheaded at his own castle of Pontefract or 'Pomfret'. His supporters, afterwards known in the records as Contrariants, are to some extent grouped in the roll under their bannerets. Any confusion may be forgiven a herald king working as a prisoner in an enemy castle, presumably Northampton, and it is not a necessary conclusion that he was as incompetent as his master. His roll is intended to be divided into sections each under a banneret, but the total of 214 knights is at this date sufficient only for a couple more than the eleven bannerets who are named upon the roll as it now is. So the roll is seen by inspection to be incomplete. Lancaster, and his father, could raise more than eleven bannerets, and many important persons are missing. Fourteen bannerets, some of them on the roll, were put to death, and eighty-six bachelors remained in prison.[1]

On the amnesty for Lancastrians in 1327 it appeared that one at least of the prisoners had been sent to Tickhill,

blazon, and even more for not distinguishing English political parties—if he *has* so failed at any point—in 1322. The terms 'Quaynté de la marmounde' and 'Bochard' (a trumpeter) are not found in other English rolls that I have examined, but the handwriting of the roll is English.

[1] A useful analysis of the personnel of both sides is given in *The Genealogist*, N.S., vol. xxi, 222–6, by the Hon. Vicary Gibbs, and this was reprinted as App. C. (pp. 597–602) in vol. ii of G.E.C. The view that the roll is a royalist one is untenable, but has misled some later writers. There was an amnesty in 1327, and the evidence of later political allegiances naturally makes nonsense of the roll.

and he was released on payment of 1,000 marks by way of fine. A couple were sent to York. Hostages, too, were kept in castles—a detestable practice for which King John had been notorious. There were in 1327 eighteen boy-hostages in Chester castle at this time, kept there to ensure the good behaviour of the Welsh. A rota, like that of castle-guard, was at this time arranged, so that six served for one week, six the second, and six the third, thus spending two weeks out of the three at home.[1] Castles, too, were still treasuries, again as in the reigns of John and Henry III.[2]

In attempting a balanced picture of the Earl of Lancaster, even Stubbs had to admit that he was 'rude, insolent, and unwarlike, an adulterer and a murderer', though Christian charity led him to add that 'he was liberal of his gifts to the poor, and a bountiful patron of the clergy: his fame grew after his death'.[3] But in life he showed up poorly by comparison with Edmund in his treatment of the town of Leicester. His behaviour is recorded in a neglected record that makes it difficult to understand how his followers could regard him, as many undoubtedly did, as a saint.[4]

On the same membrane from the sheriff's office at Northampton appears 'Le Roi Bruiant' in a list of knights bachelor who fought for Lancaster and were taken prisoner.[5] Now Lancaster, who held five earldoms, was Steward of England, so, like his predecessor Simon de Montfort (probably) and his successor and nephew Henry of Lancaster, who was also Steward, it can safely be assumed that the herald in his retinue was personal to

[1] *C. Cl. R.* (1327), 169.
[2] See J. E. A. Jolliffe on 'The Castle Treasuries' in the Powicke *Festschrift*. When Henry of Lancaster took possession of Neath Castle in Glamorgan for Edward III in 1329, he found £6,000 of Edward II's money there (*C. Cl. R.*, 445). Out of this he was able to pay John, Earl Warenne, his retaining fee of 1,600 marks—a valuable piece of information pointing to a lost indenture.
[3] W. Stubbs, *Const. Hist.* ii. 367.
[4] *Misc. Inq.* (P.R.O.), ii (1322), no. 548.
[5] D. H. Leadman, 'The Battle of Boroughbridge.' *Y.A.J.* vii (1882), 357.

him. Lancaster Herald is first found under that name in 1346–8 at the siege of Calais in the Burnell–Morley dispute, as herald of Henry of Grosmont, Earl of Lancaster (1345–61). Henry did not become Duke of Lancaster until 1351, so Lancaster Herald precedes the creation of the Duchy, and Le Roi Bruiant may be called Lancaster Herald. It will come as a surprise to many that, at so early a date, a herald king could rank with the knights bachelor.[1]

The name is known, for it was Bruiant or Bruiandiaus who in 1285, owing to his great skill in matters of arms and chivalry, told the knights assembled for the great tournament at Chauvency in Flanders who each one was.[2] The gap of thirty-seven years is a long span to be covered by one man, particularly if he was already a skilled herald in 1285 but dare not yet mingle with the knights. Yet it is by no means incredible at this time. Edward I bore arms in tournament and battle for over fifty years, and so did some of the witnesses in the Scrope–Grosvenor case. Whether two men are in question or only one, it seems that Bruant, Bruiant, or Briandiaus is a style like Norroy or Clarenceux, and not a personal name. It suggests that he was already le Roi Bruant when he joined Lancaster. Possibly, like Carlisle Herald before he was created by Edward III, he wandered about Europe finding employment where he could as a herald-ministrel, and took service with Earl Thomas in 1297–8, when the diplomatic relations between England and Flanders had reached a peak of intensity. Apart from the export of wool to Flanders, which was at its maximum a few years before the tournament of Chauvency, the two countries were linked by matrimonial ties involving the exchange

[1] Wagner, *Heralds and Heraldry* (2nd edn.), 160 (add. to p. 33 n. 2) shows that in 1332 a herald king ranked with the esquires, but in 1389 with the knights (ibid., p. 42).
[2] Wagner, *Heralds and Heraldry* (2nd edn.), p. 48, from the edn. of the Chauvency poem by Delbrouille. My reference is to p. 129, l. 306, of the poem. The editor has no comment on the origin of 'Bruiant'.

of huge diplomatic missions. In this way John, Duke of Brabant, had become Edward II's brother-in-law, one of his sisters became Countess of Bar, and John, son of Florence, Count of Holland, was another brother-in-law. There was a ministrel named Bruiant at the Swan Feast in 1306. Whether Thomas of Lancaster himself had any personal links with Flanders is not known; but he and his brother Henry, who had travelled widely in Europe before 1328, had both been fond of tournaments in their youth, and had taken part in the siege of Caerlaverock.

This roll of arms is quite incomplete, and could easily have been bettered by blazoning the shields of those on the other lists on the same document. A full roll of Lancastrian bannerets would run to twenty names, not merely the eleven that remain. Earl Thomas's predecessor had taken nineteen bannerets to Gascony with him in 1297; there were thirty bannerets and 1,500 men-at-arms with Norfolk and Hereford the same year when they refused to sail to Flanders with the king:[1] there were about 100 at Caerlaverock and at Falkirk. The remaining names are a reminder—for they include Badlesmere, Beaumont, and Roger Clifford—that in 1322 many of the royal household had deserted the king and adhered to the Lancastrian faction; not from any personal antipathy to the king, but from hatred of Isabella and Roger Mortimer. At the end even the king's gaolers at Berkeley Castle were former knights of his household, and other families for generations loyal to the Crown, such as Latimer, Pecché, and de Vere, are found on the baronial side, while Seagrave, Tyes, and la Zouche represent, one might say, the professional brawlers.

1322–4 Reforms

We can only speculate about the part played, if any, in 1322 by the country gentry in initiating or urging

[1] Hem. (old edn.), 121; Stubbs, *Select Charters*, 431–2.

administrative reform as they had done, but more in their own interest, in 1259. The knights of 1322 had all the administrative background in the shires of the *Bacheleria*: but there were, in addition, in 1322 a considerable number of very experienced M.P.s who had been elected many times, not always for the same counties, on successive occasions. If the relevant pages of the Monk of Malmesbury's detailed and authoritative narrative had not been excised or lost, we might have known the answer. The disruption of the opposition after Boroughbridge released some springs of reforming energy, which had been dammed up during Lancaster's ascendancy. The administrative reformers of these years had not the backing of a Lord Edward, as in 1259, but they had the support of the civil service: indeed, they were the civil service. The Statute of York (May 1322), the revocation of the Ordinances, the Exchequer reforms under Bishop Stapeldon of Exeter (1323–4) and under Melton (1326), the Wardrobe Ordinances under Baldock, and the Gascon Ordinances of the same period all point to detailed and extremely competent work by heads of departments acting on their own initiative.

No official source has so far revealed the status or responsibilities of the royal heralds at this time, not even the Household Ordinances, but there was a King of Arms at Boroughbridge, and he ranks with the knights bachelor.

These reforms resulted for a time in the acquisition by the Chamber of the estates of the Contrariants, for which many hundreds of *Compotus* rolls survive—the work of escheators and their clerks—,[1] and the reassertion of the authority of the Exchequer and the preservation of its records by Bishop Stapeldon of Exeter, which affected the wardrobe accounts in a number of ways, reintroducing heralds and king's messengers to exchequer accounts.

[1] Full topographical details are given in the P.R.O., *List of Ministers' Accounts* (Special Collections, No. 6).

The Statute of York (1322) recognized the Commons as an essential element in the constitution, and by its vagueness provided, like the Coronation Oath of 1308, an opportunity for extensive modern controversy, though this is not of immediate interest in the history of the chivalrous country gentry.

The obscure and sordid story of the Queen's estrangement from her husband, perhaps as much as anything through her hatred of the Despensers, and her intrigue with Roger Mortimer, forms a suitable background for the careers of self-seeking 'political bishops', leading to the tragedy of deposition, and a further period of manœuvring for power lasting until 1332.

The gradual reduction in the military, judicial, and financial duties of the sheriff was due to his executive powers falling into the hands of commissioners of array, several kinds of royal justices, tax-gatherers, and other characters in an often-told story,[1] but the sheriff remained as the chief link between local and central government; thus retaining and even accumulating a huge amount of administrative work as a returning officer with his headquarters in the shire hall, or in or near the castle. Here the sheriff had 'a permanent, efficient, and fairly numerous clerical staff'.[2] This remained, in the absence of any alternative, the repository for all local records, with the county gaol within or near by, and royal officials, including heralds, must often have had business there. This alone is sufficient to account for the at first sight odd connection between a number of rolls of arms, including the Boroughbridge and Balliol Rolls and Cooke's Ordinary, and the county courts of Northampton and Carmarthen. Even the

---

[1] Maitland, *Constitutional History*, 233: 'A very noticeable feature in English history is the decline and fall of the sheriff'; and *Justice and Police*, 69: 'Now the whole history of English Justice and Police might be brought under the rubric The Decline and Fall of the Sheriff.'

[2] See H. Jenkinson and Mabel M. Mills, 'Rolls from a Sheriff's Office in the Fourteenth Century', *E.H.R.* (Oct. 1928), 21–33; and G. H. Fowler's detailed analysis of the surviving Bedfordshire County Court Rolls.

escheators,[1] terrible men who had frequently no roots in the county, could not escape contact with the sheriff's office. Though chosen by the Crown from clerks of the royal household, they were, like forest officials or coroners, sworn in by the sheriff in the shire court.[2] From the time of Henry III the escheators and subescheators were trusted with the administration of the royal demesne, making inquisitions *post mortem*, not, like coroners, upon treasure trove or dead bodies, but upon the estates of deceased tenants-in-chief, with proofs of age and inquiries into alienation of royal demesne. They were royal stewards, explicitly so called in 1279–81. Like baronial stewards they were wide open to corruption, and a target for Ordainers.

Additions to the P.R.A.

About the time of the battle of Boroughbridge some seventy-eight names and coats of bannerets and bachelors were added to the unique manuscript of the P.R.A. They were made by a fifteenth-century scribe—witness the

[1] S. T. Gibson, 'The Escheatries, 1323–41', *E.H.R.* (1921). Some of their office-work is represented by the Special Collection, No. 6 (known as 'Ministers' Accounts' in the P.R.O.), in about 1,200 bundles of estate accounts by royal or seignorial officials often called *compotus* rolls. On the fourteenth-century escheatries see Tout, *Chapters*, iii. 49 ff., and a good summary in Lodge and Thornton, *Constitutional Documents* (1935), 356. The key references to the early history of the office are *C.P.R.* (1348), 6, and *C. Cl. R.* (1248), 105, 138–9.

[2] For the swearing-in, see *Cal. F.R.* (1272), 1. From 1248–9 the realm was divided into two provinces, North and South of Trent, referred to in royal writs as *citra* and *ultra Trentan*, but as from the location of the royal court at any given moment: i.e. if you wish to write to an escheator in Kent from the Exchequer when it is at York, he is *ultra Trentan*. In time of stress there was much chopping and changing of their numbers and spheres of authority. The escheators best known to me were clerks: Mr. Richard de Clifford (South of Frent, 1272–4); Mr. Henry de Bray, whose 'estate book' of private memoranda has been published by the Camden Society and used effectively by Sir Maurice Powicke, *Medieval England* (Home University Library); and Mr. Walwayn, of whom I have written at length in *E.H.R.* (1956) but Sir William Trussel, of parliamentary fame, was very definitely a knight of the royal household.

ink—[1]but from an earlier source: probably another copy of the P.R.A. that had been modernized in the last decade of Edward II's reign. It is found by comparison with the retinues at the Dunstable tournament, which shows, for example, four Darcys and five Latimers, that many of the additions were made in the Lancastrian interest. A number of them were M.P.s in the time of Edward II[2] and some of them rebelled with Henry of Lancaster in 1328–9. A comparison of the additions with the Boroughbridge Roll shows the Lancastrian character of each. These Lancastrian families of the time of Edward II were not necessarily of the same persuasion in the fifteenth century. The late Mr. K. B. McFarlane has shown that there was no continuity of faction among the gentry in the Lancastrian period, but the considerations adduced by him do not apply to a period before the later fourteenth century.[3]

These additions to the P.R.A. led to an enlarged version, known as B, to which some further twenty names had been added. B appears to be based on a lost manuscript in which Thomas de Brotherton, the Earl Marshal (d. 1338), and the Earl of Kent (forfeited and executed in 1330) were the two chief additions, but Suffolk and Norfolk are amplified. This enlarged version begins with James Butler, Earl of Ormonde. The original of B was owned by Thomas of Lancaster, Duke of Clarence (1411–21), and Constable of the Army in 1417. Brotherton, although he was once fined for negligence, may have inspired this version, as his interest in his duties may be thought to be reflected in the tract entitled 'Les Usages de

---

[1] These additions were italicized by Mr. Oswald Barron in his edition, and it was he who pointed to their date. The marginal crosses referring to deceased persons could be late Edward II. One, *P.R.A.* 373 (Bucks.), is for John de Olneye (d. 1325–6). The Clarendon type used for these marks in *Parl. Writs* makes them far more conspicuous than they are in the manuscripts.

[2] Robert Aspele, Robert de Curzon, William de Dene, Roger Maudiut, William le Moigne, John de Munteney, William de Paris, Peter de Saltmarsh, Robert Walkfare, John de Whelwetham, John de Zefoul, were M.P.s *temp.* Edward II.

[3] K. B. McFarlane, *The Wars of the Roses* (Ralegh Lecture, 1964).

M. Thomas de Brotherton'. This version (?1337–8) was again revised after 1340 to include Henry, first Lord Scrope of Masham, as Le Seigneur de Scrope, with some other *post*-1360 names.[1]

The Marshal is something of a problem at this period, because Brotherton is the Marshal in fee until his death in 1339, and after this date the office in fee is held by a lady who lived until 1399. It is not always easy to determine who was the acting Marshal after 1338, or even before.[2] Another Marshal was created to replace Brotherton; this was William de Montacute, recently created Earl of Salisbury, who was appointed Marshal of England for life by patent dated 20 September 1339 at Antwerp. Montacute died on 20 January 1344, from bruises, it is said, received at the tournament of Windsor. No known roll of arms seems to be associated with him.

It will be clear to those who are acquainted with the Marshal's perquisites that the cry 'Marshal, give me a horse' of the William the Marshal poem of the early thirteenth century is a piece of licensed jesting by the herald-ministrel, for everyone knew that the Marshal collected a fine horse from each newly created baron. It is obvious from the wardrobe account of Edward I's reign that the heralds are in the Marshal's department at court, but it is equally clear from later records that they are not regarded as part of the establishment, and I do not know whether or not they received annual robes and fees from the Wardrobe after the time of Edward I. They seem to drift 'out of court'. The *N.E.D.* states that the Marshal appoints the king's heralds. I do not find any fourteenth-century authority for this statement. Nor do I know how any fourteenth-century herald became entitled to function unless by royal or seignorial appointment. 'Les

---

[1] See *C.E.M.R.A.* 46–7 for further textual details.

[2] In 1337 the Earl Marshal had a Knight Marshal deputy, John de Leukenore, in the royal household at 2*s*. a day when the Earl was at court, and 4*s*. when the Earl was out of court (*C. Cl. R.* (20 June 1337), 79).

Usages' throws no light on this:[1] there is in this undated compilation no word of heralds or heraldry.[2]

The Marshal in this period still had the right not only to a palfrey from each new abbot who held by barony, but to 100*s*. from each new baron, that is he took a shilling in the pound on every baronial relief,[3] and was probably entitled to charge new earls at the same rate.

The brief treatise on the office of Marshal in Cott. MS. Nero D, vi (? about A.D. 1400), is preceded by a charter of the king dated 12 January Ric. II granting in fee to Thomas, Earl of Nottingham, and his heirs male the name, honour, and office of Marshal of England. This is followed by the heading *Ces somt les Usages de Thomas de Brotherton filx au Roy clamoit a user par loffice mareschalsie*. This may be of the second quarter of the fourteenth century, for Brotherton was Marshal from 1312 to 1338. The first paragraph is in Latin, the rest in Anglo-Norman, and in fact deals also with duties and perquisites of the Constable as well as the Marshal. After a page or two of this there is a final paragraph in Latin on the duties of the Marshal in time of peace, especially at court, and within the verge, where he acts through a clerk and a sergeant.

This tract attests the increased interest at that time in the technique of government and in the technique of heraldry, parallel to the revivals in our own time of interest in the king's government at work and the efflorescence of heraldic studies.

[1] Brotherton was perhaps inadequate. He was fined £100 in 1323 for not appointing a deputy to attend the judges in eyre in Lancashire (*C. Cl. R.* (19 Nov. 1323), 144–5).

[2] That the Earl Marshal himself had a herald is obvious, but the fact is not mentioned until 1334, when a gift of 40*s*. from the king is recorded. *Johanni Johnet heralds armorum Comitis Marescalli*, in a Wardrobe Account (P.R.O. 101/387/9 under 7 May 1334). This roll also mentions John Teirsaunte as a royal herald of arms who received £6 a year for his robes in 1332–4.

[3] *Ann. Dunst.* 412. The Earl of Warwick, Thomas de Beauchamp, who was Marshal *quamdiu* took a case concerning the abbey of Dunstable to the court of the Steward and Marshal, claiming that the fee was due if they held even by parcel of a barony, but a jury of the neighbourhood at St. Albans said that all that the abbot had was held in free alms and not by barony.

Richard de Bury even coined a word *Panfletus*[1] to describe the occasional studies to which the movement gave birth. At the head must stand the controversial *Modus tenendi Parliamentum*, and the tracts associated with Andrew Horn, the Chamberlain of London (d. 1329), i.e. the 'Mirror of Justices', and other pseudo-historical works, such as those of enigmatic Britton. These tractates have in common a strong political bias. While pretending to expound the facts the authors managed to insert a certain whimsicality and unreality into the proceedings. The treatise on the Steward embodied and expanded the Lancastrian claim to that office, and has been dated 1321.[2]

The heralds themselves may have noticed the increased use of inescutcheons attested by the Boroughbridge Roll.[3] The *faux escutcheon*, or, in the later phrase, 'shield of pretence', is found on our earliest extant roll for Balliol (Glover's Roll Nos. 30, 86, 87), Bertram (No. 139), Lindsay (No. 200), Monchesney (No. 25), and Mortimer (No. 32), and leads to the reflection that heraldry owes as much to the Marchers as to the Crusaders, and that the earliest recorded shields are charged not with crosses but with chevrons.

Another technicality that intrudes itself at this time is whether the proper description of that royal beast in the zoo in the Tower of London was a lion or a leopard. The Chancery was uncertain. The truth may be that the animal was itself in doubt, because if it looked at you when in passing it was (or became) a leopard, otherwise it was a lion. It had a good appetite: a quarter of mutton daily, costing from $2\frac{1}{2}d.$ to $6d.$—depending on the price of meat.[4] They should have sent for a herald to see if it

---

[1] The word is first found in the *Philobiblon* (A.D. 1345).

[2] M. V. Clarke, *Representation and Consent*, 242–3.

[3] Danvers (46), Turpinton (55), Enpingham (82), Vauz (127), Blanchfroun with the Mortimer inescutcheon (150), Percehay with Aton inescutcheon (154), Cramville (192), and Darcy le Fiz (204).

[4] *C. Cl. R.* (1313–18), 4, 60, 124, 163. The distinction is made in P.R.A. 912 (Ludlow), and P.R.A. 115 (Tregoz of Sussex) has a golden leopard passing by which the earlier rolls (Glover, Collins, St. George, and Dering) call a lion.

would look at him, as the kings of arms had already decided that if it did it was not a lion but a leopard. Lesser heralds do not seem to have heard of this decision.

It sometimes happened that men who inherited dignities had two coats of arms. Hence the utility of the lists of deceased earls that head so many rolls of arms: someone will marry the heiress to the *caput* of the fief and become entitled to the use of the arms attached to the dignity. Simon de Montfort, Earl of Leicester and Steward of England, was an instance of this.[1] The same is noted in the history of other sergeanties.

The Marmion family held the Norman barony of Fontenay by being hereditary champions of the Dukes. William the Conqueror gave Lutterworth, Scrivelsby, and Tamworth Castle to Robert de Marmion for the same service. On the death in 1292 of Philip Marmion, last male of his line, who left only daughters, Tamworth fell to the Frevilles; Scrivelsby, the *caput*, went to his daughter Margaret Ludlow, and her daughter in turn married Sir John Dymoke, who thus became champion, as holder of the *caput* to which the sergeanty was attached. Marmion had a coat as champion, *azure a sword erect argent hilted or*, and his family arms were *vair a fess gules*.[2] The family were much involved in the affairs of William, Earl of Aumale, his countess Isabella de Fortibus, and Adam de Stratton in the period 1260–72.[3]

[1] *History and Heraldry*, 44–5.

[2] Dering roll No. 174. The whole story is given in *D.N.B.*, s.v. Dymoke. The sword on the Dering roll is given as black, but presumably only because the tincture is tarnished. The family arms are in Glover (No. 46 for William Marmion, No. 56 for Philip); and Dering, No. 89, Collins, No. 169, P.R.A. No. 63 for John, M.P. for Lincs., May 1298. The William Marmion who was knighted in May 1306 (Ashmole No. 253) is P.R.A. No. 823 (Leics.), was M.P. for his county in 1307, and is No. 199 on the first Dunstable roll.

[3] After 1260 William Marmion the elder was one of the Earl's executors. He thus appears in the Fortibus estate accounts, sometimes with William *Minor* or *le cosin*, sometimes with Manasser Marmion. On one occasion a gift of 12 deer was sent to Amice Marmion. See also *Reg. Gravesend*, 38, 223, showing a gift of the rectory of Coningsby in 1269 by Philip Marmion to Adam de Stratton, who was guardian of the heir of William Marmion in 1272.

IV

ROLLS OF ARMS OF EDWARD III's REIGN (1327–1377)

1. Second Dunstable Tournament Roll, January 1334
2. Balliol Roll, June 1334
3. Ashmole Roll XV A, December 1334–February 1335
4. Carlisle Roll, 12 July 1335
5. Cotgrave's Ordinary, before 1340
6. Cooke's Ordinary, c. 1340
7. Powell's Roll, c. 1350

   The purpose and content of this chapter is primarily to date and localize the above-listed rolls of arms.

8. William Jenyns's Ordinary, c. 1380

KING EDWARD III was knighted on 1 February 1327, the eve of his coronation, at the age of 15 or 16 when he was old enough to bear arms in practice as well as in theory, just as his grandfather the Lord Edward had been in 1254. He had the misfortune to come to the throne at a time when those who would inevitably oppose him were firmly in the saddle, but he celebrated his coming of military age with a *chevauchée*, which may be put side by side with the Lord Edward's initiation into the military art at the tournament of Blyth in Yorkshire. His grandson went still further north and, presumably with the acquiescence of Mortimer (in power 1327–30), attempted to break a lance with the Scots at Stanhope Park in Northumberland, whither they had advanced to meet him. Professor McKisack points out that the young aspirant (or *tiro*, as Matthew Paris said of his grandfather) to military honours returned 'deeply humilitated'. It certainly did nothing to quench his thirst for military glory.

At Northampton next year, Mortimer came to terms with the Scots, and the Lancastrian attainder was reversed in Parliament. Henry of Lancaster, Earl Thomas's younger brother, now old and almost blind, was still dissatisfied with the regime, and staged a demonstration in the Lancastrian tradition at Bedford.

The king's personal rule begins with his dramatic assumption of power in October 1330 by a *coup d'état* arranged with the aid of Montague, who became Earl of Salisbury, and Richard de Bury. For the next thirty-five years Edward reigned in majesty and with great success. He was blessed with a supremely happy marriage, which also brought him the services of Walter Mauny, a Fleming, who in 1330 transferred from the Queen's household to that of Edward himself. Both Edward and Mauny tasted the beginnings of military fame in Scotland in 1332, and Edward had already shown unusual political shrewdness in granting an amnesty to his opponents and arranging for *querele* into local government, at the same time ordering the complete and permanent removal of the existing sheriffs. His creation in 1337 of the three new earldoms of Huntingdom for Clinton, Northampton for Bohun, and Salisbury for Montague is a reminder that with the exception of de la Pole, who becomes Suffolk under Richard II in 1386 and the first merchant to become an earl, fourteenth-century promotions are from ancient families. It was Henry I who had raised men such as the Clintons, the Bassets, and the Trussebuts 'from the dust to do his service'.[1]

Hugh Courtenay the elder, Earl of Devon, seems to have been reluctant to assume the style of earl, though he entered upon the inheritance of the last Countess, Isabella de Forz (d. 1293), by hereditary right. When he did so the king resumed payment, which had been withheld for some

[1] Ordericus Vitalis, *Eccl. hist.*, lib. xi, cap. 2.

OF EDWARD III'S REIGN, 1327–1377   91

time on account of his behaviour, of the third penny (amounting to £18. 6s. 8d.) of the profits of justice in the county, extended at £55. Hugh had received it on the death of the Countess for some time, *and it was detained from him because he had not been styled earl*, so the sheriff was ordered to make proclamation in the county court and in other places in that bailiwick that all should recognize Hugh as Earl of Devon, 'because the king has ordered him to assume that name and honour'.[1]

Edward III's national and mercantilist policy, his re-establishment of the Staple at Calais in 1346 to keep the carrying trade in English hands, the encouragement of weaving in England, and his sumptuary legislation, as in Italian cities,[2] with regulation of labour, are not to be taken as evidence of a leaning towards a totalitarian or fascist state grappling with a hostile and at times communistic peasantry. Such interpretations are outside the scope of this book and do not advance knowledge, for it is vain to speak of the fourteenth or any other century in terms of the twentieth. Edward was far more able, just as unscrupulous, and a much better general than used to be admitted; not, indeed, either a fascist or a totalitarian, but very much a man of his age, and for long the mirror of chivalry. His troops, their generals, and his commissariat were trained in the Scottish wars. His efforts to distrain men to become knights far exceeded anything that Edward I had attempted, but the extent to which they were successful has not been a subject of comment. We do not know how many men took up knighthood because they were forced so to do, and how many escaped the net.[3]

[1] *C. Cl. R.* (22 Feb. 1335), 466, also in *Foedera*. No explanation is given of this unusual behaviour.

[2] See H. Kantorowicz and N. Denholm-Young, 'De Ornatu Mulierum', *Bibliofilia* (Olschki, Florence, 1933).

[3] A series of eight writs between 20 Mar. 1333 and 2 July 1335 were intended to force all men who had had £40 a year in hand or rents for three years to become knights, in preparation for the great muster on 12 July 1335. Even Durham and Chester were dragged in (*C. Cl. R.* (1333–7), 93, 123, 142, 144,

A general impression left by the mass of administrative detail contained in the chancery enrolments of the three Edwards is that Edward III planned the financing and victualling of his armies and fleets with much greater attention to practical detail than Edward I had done. There is none of the ordering of impossible numbers of men to be impressed or incredible amounts of provisions to be purveyed. Much more authority was given to the man on the spot to organize supplies as efficiently as he could. Edward's agents for this purpose were new men, at the outbreak of war men like William Fraunk and Walter Mauny. The degree of efficiency with which the king inspired his local agents in the first twenty years of his reign is quite remarkable. He was building on a solid foundation of administrative achievement laid by Edward I which the ineffectiveness and near-anarchy of much of his father's reign had failed to destroy, and the achievements that followed were worthy of the efforts made.

The 1336 campaign in Scotland is not important from a military point of view,[1] but it was at this time that king and Council decided to set on foot preparations for a defensive war against France, and the war manifesto usually dated late August 1337 had already been decided upon on or before 6 August 1336 at Perth.[2] On that day John of Norwich was appointed Admiral of the Fleet from the Thames to the north and sent with a small force *prepared to war* to intercept French galleys sending aid to the Scots.[3] In the autumn (4 November 1336) at Stirling, Geoffrey de Say was appointed as the other admiral, his command extending from the Thames to the

211, 362, and 418, and (1337–9), 184), and the younger Droxford relentlessly pursued.

[1] It is not noticed in Professor McKisack's *The Fourteenth Century*.
[2] *Foed.* ii. 994–5. Misdated.
[3] *C. Cl. R.* (1336), 606–7. Payments authorized on and after 6 Aug. to John of Norwich for wages (the army at sea was paid at the same rate as it was on land) and victuals. Note that men-at-arms (at a shilling a day) now include esquires.

west,[1] and on the same day Richard de Bury, now Bishop of Durham, was sent to treat with Philip of France. As the Council had already in August decided that war with France was inevitable, this was obviously a blind, and Bury clearly the man to manipulate it. After a meteoric rise he was at the peak of his career as a diplomat, a man (as readers of his *Philobiblon* will remember) adept at saying nothing gracefully and at considerable length. At this point Edward and his advisers seemed to have thought of the now inevitable war as purely defensive. For French aid to Scotland was not just an excuse for war, it was a primary and valid reason. The Valois was just as ambitious as Edward, and the transfer of the French fleet from the Mediterranean to the Channel constituted a real threat to everything that Edward had already achieved in the north. The king may have thought in 1336 that he had settled the Scottish problem for a time, as his grandfather had thought in 1305, but this time with infinitely less trouble. In 1336 the administrative machine swung into high gear with great smoothness. Edward III was, if anything, better served on land, at sea, and at home than Edward I had been. He retained—after one scandal leading to the Walton Ordinances in 1340—the loyalty not only of his generals but of his administrators for twenty years. After Brétigny all is anti-climax.

The practice, already firmly entrenched in the thirteenth century, of rewarding household knights and others with nominal custodies of castles or counties[2] was continued by Edward III. William de Clinton, for example, was made Constable of Dover and Warden of the Cinque Ports long before he was created an earl. Walter Mauny, for services rendered in Scotland, received about £750 for the next thirty years as life-sheriff of Merioneth, the whole of North Wales being at that time worth about £3,000 to

---

[1] *C. Cl. R.* (1336), 623 (4 Nov. at Stirling).
[2] For nominal castellans see the introduction to the *Caerlaverock Poem*, ed. N. Denholm-Young and C. Bullock Davies (forthcoming).

the king. Mauny was made sheriff in 1332, when he had been in England five years. He had arrived from Flanders with Queen Isabella at the age of 17, and remained in office for forty years, 'without having, so far as I know, entered the County of Merioneth, or the castle of Harlech of which he was constable'.[1] Most of the sheriffs were English, except Sir Griffith Llwyd, a faithful supporter of Edward I and Edward II. In 1327 Wales sent twenty-four M.P.s to Westminster, but Sir Griffith 'refused to come to witness the king's degradation'. There were no more Welsh M.P.s till 1536. In 1337 Mauny was allowed by Edward III £8,000 for ransoms for the release of prisoners. He was not at Crécy, but from 1346 he was summoned to Parliament by writ as Lord Mauny. He was a man of eminent piety, who bought thirteen acres in Smithfield as a mass burial-ground for victims of the Black Death in 1349,[2] and founded the Charterhouse in Smithfield in 1370. He died in 1372.

It was the appointment of such non-resident sheriffs and justices in the fourteenth and fifteenth centuries that led to the rise of the Welsh gentry in Tudor times. The earliest of them formed a sizeable group descended from the same stock as Ednyfed Fychan, seneschal to Llewelyn the Great and his son David (from about 1216 to his death in 1246), by 1282 a large and powerful class. Professor Glyn Roberts has described Fychan as the ancestor of a great number of medieval and modern gentry families.[3] Another group was formed by the ancestors of Vaughan of Corsygedol in Merionethshire, who leased Crown revenues and farmed the shrievalty.

[1] D. L. Evans, 'Walter de Mauny, Sheriff of Merioneth, 1332-72', *Journal of the Merioneth Hist. and Rec. Soc.*, vol. iv, pt. iii, 194-203. A delightful paper.

[2] It was as a result of the Black Death that the great Record of Caernarvon was made in 1352. The original is at U.C.N.W., Bangor, among the Baron Hill MSS. of the Bulkeley family who lived there, near Beaumaris. It was edited for the Record Commission by Sir Henry Ellis in 1838 from the Harl. MSS. in the British Museum.

[3] Glyn Roberts, 'Wales and England', *Welsh History Review*, vol. i, No. 4 (1963), 379.

These men fought in France under Edward III and the Black Prince, and were in the personal service of Richard II. Some of this may have been due to the deliberate policy of the Crown in suggesting that trusted officials should do everything in their power to persuade influential Welshmen to send some of their children to be of the king's household[1]—thus repeating Archbishop Pecham's advice of a previous generation. Edward II as Prince from 1301 had had, as seen in the Kennington petitions of 1305, a considerable number of Welsh officials, though not as constables,[2] in Wales and in his own household.

Much had been achieved by intermarriage. Llewelyn the Great had married a daughter of King John, and five of his sons and daughters married into English baronial families. His grandson Llewelyn the Last had married Eleanor, daughter of Simon de Montfort. His line ended in an heiress who as a royal ward was married to John Cherleton of Shropshire, founding the line of Cherleton and Grey Lord of Powys which lasted into the Tudor period.

The innate hostility of Welsh to Saxon persisted in the fourteenth century and, except among 'London Welsh' and sections of the gentry, for long after. In the fifteenth century the rise of the gentry as a class seems to follow the same pattern with a time-lag as in England. The whole culture of Wales, as reflected in the handwriting of the surviving manuscripts, was archaic. Apart from the Black Prince's Register and the Record of Caernarvon, and material to be gathered piecemeal from English record sources, there is a great lack of information on Welsh society between 1327 and 1377. There are no chronicles, and there is no register for South Wales to solve for us the tantalizing problem of Cooke's Ordinary from

[1] Op. cit., 381; citing J. G. Edwards, *Cal. Anct. Corr. relating to Wales*, 253–4.
[2] An ordinance of Edward I, alluded to in *B.P.R.* i. 159, *s.a.* 1348, provided that no Welshman was to hold a castle or other 'office of charge', and one who had been appointed in Cardiganshire was to be dismissed.

Carmarthen. There is in the Marcher areas, as Professor Glyn Roberts remarked, 'a pattern of co-operation punctuated, as in the Principality, by periodic spasms of racial hatred and rebellion'.[1]

It is a crying fault among English historians that they pay only lip-service to the fact that the Tudors, who came from a farmhouse at Penmynydd in Angelsey, were a typically Welsh family, and it is time for their conquest of England in 1485 to be described with this in mind.

The Four Rolls of 1334–1335

These four rolls have been indexed, and it is hoped to publish the result separately as a Who's Who for 1334–5, or a Peerage, Baronage, and Knightage of England on the eve of the Hundred Years War. They have been fully described by Sir Anthony Wagner in his *Catalogue* and may now be dated as follows:

II Dunst. or the Second Dunstable Roll, January 1334.
Balliol Roll, June 1334.
Ashmolean Roll 15A, December 1334–February 1335.
Carlisle Roll 12, July 1335.

These are accurately dated and contain little that is not completely contemporary (though Piers Gaveston, who died in 1312, is on the Ashmolean Roll).

The key to these rolls is that for the sake of the Scottish campaigns the seat of government was moved from Westminster in 1332 to York, where it remained for five years, until 1338.[2] The rolls in consequence contain an unusually high proportion of northern names. The little heraldic treatise that precedes the transcript of the

---

[1] Glyn Roberts, op. cit., p. 386. A beginning was made by D. L. Evans in 'Some Notes on the History of the Principality in the time of the Black Prince', *Trans. Hon. Soc. of Cymmrodorion* (1925–6), 25–100.

[2] The same transfer had been made for similar reasons from 9 June 1297 to Christmas 1304.

Ashmolean Roll could have been made at or near York between 1332 and 1338.¹

These years of annual campaigns, nominally in support of Edward Balliol against the Scots, saw the compilation of four rolls of arms. Though Balliol was crowned in 1332 he did not do homage till 19 June 1334 at Newcastle, when Andrew Clarenceux and his fellow heralds made minstrelsy before the king and were given fifty marks.² It is to this latter date that I assign the Balliol Roll, a list of thirty-five Scottish lords and knights, 'perhaps actual or potential adherents of Edward Balliol'.³ The roll is not the 'oldest known collection of Scottish arms', a title awarded by Sir James Ramsay to the Ragman Roll of 1296.⁴

The second document is the Dunstable tournament roll of (probably) 20–23 January 1334, when the magnates from London and the south came to meet the king returning victorious after the Halidon Hill campaign. This too is a comparatively small list of 135 names and blazoned arms, which has come down to us in sixteenth- and seventeenth-century copies. There was a large number of king's knights among the contestants, and it was the first royal tournament since the king had taken control of the government. It may be assumed that this roll was made on the spot.

The third is a fifteenth-century copy of a much longer roll, and it is a much greater problem.⁵ It can be dated

---

¹ H. Stanford London, 'Early Treatises on Heraldry', *The Antiquaries Journal*, vol. xxxiii (1953).

² Brit. Mus. Add. MS. 46350 (a wardrobe account for 1332) cited by Wagner, p. 159, says 'on the day the king of Scotland did homage'. A similar entry is on the Counter Roll under 19 June 1334 in P.R.O. E. 101/387/9.

³ *C.E.M.R.A.*, p. 54, where the roll is assigned to *c.* 1332, the year of Balliol's coronation. I do not know of any rolls drawn up at coronations. It could be so, but this is a roll of English not Scottish provenance, endorsed upon Cooke's Ordinary.

⁴ 'The Ur-armorial of the Scottish gentry', Ramsay, *Dawn of the Constitution*, p. 433, n. 5: The cognisances of the leading Scottish families are all there, the Murray Stars, the Stewart Fess, the Graham Scallop-shell, etc.

⁵ Bod. Lib. Ashm. roll 15A. It also contains a brief treatise on heraldry, and a list of lords beginning with the Earl of Huntingdon, one of the

neatly between December 1334 and January 1335, but it is not, like the three others, an occasional roll, and there are a few names upon it of deceased persons. For the most part it seems to have been made at or near York and to contain persons who were there or passed through on their way to the north. This roll is clearly linked with Cotgrave's Ordinary, made a few years later. The fourth roll is also a fifteenth-century copy, but it is a portion of a larger roll of great interest. This is the Carlisle Roll of 12 July 1335, perhaps the sole tangible relic of Edward III's greatest, and least effective, effort against the Scots, a record of one of the largest armies he ever mustered.

The Ashmolean Roll needs further consideration.[1] In many instances where an alternative description would not excite surprise, there is an exact similarity to the blazon used in Cotgrave. Both rolls are using for 90 per cent of their entries, strictly contemporary material. Both are strong where the P.R.A. is weak, in the northern counties.

There is a possibility that the compiler of Cotgrave had access to a copy of the Ashmolean Roll, and it further seems likely that Cotgrave's Ordinary is earlier than Cooke's. This view is based on grounds of general historical probability that, where two roughly contemporary documents have at least 75 per cent of their subject-matter in common, the shorter version is likely to be the

creations of 1337. As William de Clinton, Constable of Dover and Warden of the Cinque Ports from 1333, Huntingdon could have had a herald, and this list could be the first stage in the construction of a roll of arms—the collection of names to be included for the newly created earl, who may have taken or been granted the style to assert Edward III's claims upon Scotland as Balliol's suzerain. The date, assigned by Sir Anthony Wagner, seems to depend upon the absence from the list of the Earl of Courteney, created Earl of Devon 22 Feb. 1335, and also upon the presence of someone who could not occur before 17 Oct. 1334. The roll, described in Black's quarto *Catal of the Ash. MSS. in the Bod. Lib.*, 7, is of six membranes joined chancery fashion.

[1] The roll is the work of a good penman, but a poor copyist. A peculiarity is that he always writes 'lipard' for 'lupard'. There are some very strange spellings where he is unfamiliar with names that meant little in the fifteenth century, for example, le Conte de Garrenul, plainly written, for Garenne (or Warenne).

earlier—even if, as is quite possible, they were produced independently one of another. The idea that the charges upon a series of shields could and should be arranged in a logical order is unfortunately the work of an anonymous herald, but it is one of those simple strokes of genius in classification, more important than alphabetical order, without which there could be no science of heraldry. The Ashmolean Roll, however, undoubtedly has its roots in Yorkshire,[1] with a few coats from Westmorland, Nottinghamshire, and Lincolnshire. If a man lived further away he was sometimes singled out as 'Mr. Touchet of Derbyshire', Beaumont of Devon, Verdon of Derbyshire, Coleville of Cambridgeshire. There are a few Cornishmen (M.P.s at York in 1324). A few doubtful instances occur where only the family name is given, so that it is uncertain whether a lord or a knight is in question. The totals comprise a dozen earls, forty-eight lords, and some 406 knights.

The scribe of this fifteenth-century roll was something of a sociologist. The original was a manuscript of 1334–5, but in the period between that date and the date of this copy some families had risen, others had sunk. This seems to be the explanation of a certain disorder in the roll. Two persons styled Mr. Hugh de Audley and Fulk Fitzwarin are among the lords, and nine lords are among the knights.[2] Being a true herald and not an historian the scribe has changed the style of these men to bring his roll up to date.

By 1334 Edward III, at the age of 21, had been his own master for four years. A little group of the king's friends led by Richard de Bury and William Montague, created Earl of Salisbury for his help, had put the king

[1] The tractate on heraldry in the same manuscript is certainly a northern product, for in speaking of bastardy it refers to the practice of heralds 'down in the Southourn contrewe'.

[2] Coleville and Cobham, Nos. 75–6; Hilton and Morley, Nos. 84–5; Huntercombe, No. 106; Hussey and Stopham, Nos. 161, 167; William de Weston and Leutoft or Lentoft, Nos. 237, 238.

hors de page, as Edmund Burke said of another occasion in the reign of George III. Edward's personal rule had then begun and by 1334 the country was on the way to recovering its lost prestige and financial solvency, though this was not fully achieved until 1337–8, when it had become possible to finance a war through native and not Italian agents.

The story of Edward's martial exploits brings us within the orbit of the Flemish writer Froissart, whose stories of battles won by individual heroism, or vows accomplished by noble deeds, are the work of an artist. He was also a poet, the son of a herald-painter, who wrote at the end of the fourteenth century and died about 1410. He was in his teens when he first visited England and became one of Queen Philippa of Hainault's secretaries in 1361. He was still only 28 when he left England for Brussels to attend an international conference of minstrels. Such as he was in youth, he tells us, so he remained in old age—a child at heart, and one who cared little for precision in matters of dates or numbers. As he had only just been born when the Hundred Years War broke out, Froissart had to take the earlier part of his chronicle wholesale from that of Jean le Bel, canon of Liège, who covered the period 1326 to 1361, dying in 1370. Much of medieval chivalry was consciously invented by Edward III, with his Round Table, joustings, and chivalrous order of international fame, but it was the Burgundian writers in Flanders who preserved it for us.[1]

The romantic period of ponderous knights on Flemish stallions and the supremacy of the English yeomanry as mounted archers was ushered in by the defeat of the Scots at Halidon Hill in 1333, a dress rehearsal for Crécy eleven years later; and the greatest army ever

[1] The standard editions of Froissart are by Kervyn de Lettenhove (25 volumes, Brussels, 1867–77) and S. Luce and G. Raynaud for the Société de l'Histoire de France (11 volumes to 1385, Paris 1869–99). The English translation by Lord Berners, edited by W. P. Ker in 6 volumes (Tudor Translations) was reissued in 8 volumes in 1927–8.

assembled by Edward III,[1] with one or two possible exceptions, mustered at Newcastle on 12 July 1335, and saw the creation of Carlisle Herald, as well as the now fragmentary Carlisle roll of arms. On this occasion Edward III overran the Lowlands of Scotland, but no great feat of arms resulted.

The creation of Carlisle Herald is Edward's first conscious step on the road to military glory. The story is told from Froissart by Sir Anthony Wagner, who assigns it to 1327. The herald had on his own statement, as reported in the chronicle, which at this point is copying Jean de Bel, been abroad five years before his return to England on 13 April 1338, the year of Froissart's birth. The creation of Carlisle Herald had taken place before he left, and it would be natural to associate it with Halidon Hill in 1333. But great battles do not necessarily produce great rolls, or any rolls at all, e.g. there is none of Evesham, Crécy, or Poitiers. The scene of heraldic activities is the castle rather than the camp, and heralds are diplomatic envoys not strenuous knights. Even at Falkirk, where a king of arms is known to have been in Sir Henry Percy's retinue, it is not suggested that he was on the field of battle. So the assignment of Carlisle Herald to the Carlisle muster of 1335 is possible, though the date is a year out, for five years back from 1338 takes us, counting as the Romans once did, and as the French still do,[2] to 1334. But Edward *was* at Carlisle in July 1335 and not in 1334 and the Count of Juliers who is on the roll was with the army this year and no other.[3]

The present Carlisle Roll was made in the mid fifteenth

[1] A. E. Prince, 'The Strength of English Armies in the Reign of Edward III', *E.H.R.* xliv (1931), 353–71, especially 356. The wages bill amounted to £12,000.

[2] e.g. 'the octave or the quinzaine of a feast', and 'huit jours' and 'quinze jours' for a week or fortnight.

[3] The Count of Juliers was the Queen's brother-in-law. He had had a pension of 900 marks a year since 1333. In Dec. 1335 he went home. Details are in *C. Cl. R.* (1335), 458, 527, 535. William V of Juliers is No. 241 and his retinue Nos. 242–75.

century as a painted version of a blazoned occasional roll made, according to the heading, on '12 July in the eighth year' when the king was leading his army into Scotland. This is an impossible statement. On that date the king was at or near Nottingham and not on his way to Scotland. Secondly, internal evidence shows that the ninth not the eighth year is in question. For the roll undoubtedly shows part of the army of 12 July 1335. Whoever named it 'the Carlisle Roll' must have realized this, though it is not at all obvious from the roll where the muster took place. However, since it is to be dated 12 July 1335, it may still be called the Carlisle Roll, for the king was there on that day, before setting out with some 15,000 men all told on a magnificent but futile march through the Lowlands of Scotland. The more obvious clues to the date and place of the roll are the appearance of the Count of Juliers and his followers, and of Sir Eustace Maxwell and one or two others who are known from records of the royal household to have been present on this occasion. Regnal years are always confusing, and at some stage in the transmission of this roll 1335 has been described as *oitisme* instead of *neuvisme* or *neufisme* or some such word. Sir Anthony Wagner in his *C.E.M.R.A.* does not say how or when the name Carlisle came to be attached to the roll, but in view of the misleading heading it was an inspired choice of names.

The Carlisle Roll was clearly intended to be a large one, presumably of the cavalry in battle array after the great muster at Carlisle on 12 July, when David Bruce and Joan his wife had been driven out of Scotland and Edward III marched to the rescue of the harassed Balliol. The remaining portion of the roll gives only part of the army. This extant fragment contains two earls, thirteen bannerets, and 262 knights, led by Humphrey, Earl of Hereford, the Constable. The Constables of England in the fourteenth and fifteenth centuries became much more prominent in relation to the other earls than they had been in the thirteenth century. If the muster at Newcastle followed known precedents there would have been from sixty to seventy-five bannerets in all; fewer than at Falkirk or Caerlaverock, but the proportion of bannerets to their troops had much lessened, and the number of mounted archers, now a decisive factor, had vastly increased.

As the roll is not complete it must remain a moot point how much of the army it is really intended to represent. It is known from the wardrobe accounts that there were 50 bannerets and 450 knights in this army, but there are only 277 knights, bannerets, and foreigners on this roll, i.e. rather less than half the total of native knights, but clearly much more than a vanguard. The army is known to have advanced into Scotland in two columns and it may be that this is a complete roll in itself of the column with the vanguard and the king; or it may be that the roll was not made at Carlisle, but at Newcastle-on-Tyne, where the muster had been at midsummer, and that this roll is an incomplete one of the army before it split into two, the one column advancing into Scotland from Newcastle under Warenne (naturally not on this roll) and the other with the king marching across to Carlisle and thence into the Lowlands by way of Erthe or Erd and to Perth, where, I think, they joined, and so home again. They probably returned because the king and his advisers were seriously alarmed at the manœuvres of the French king and his fleet.[1]

The heading of the roll seems to be a fifteenth-century addition, because it states that Edward III advanced into Scotland with two earls and thirteen bannerets, and this is quite certainly only a part of the story, which was apparently unknown to whoever wrote the heading. He says 'two earls' because as it stands the roll names only

[1] The Scottish campaigns are admirably dealt with by Dr. Ranald Nicholson, *Edward III and the Scots* (Oxford, 1965), though this roll of arms is not mentioned. See especially Chaps. XIII and XIV, for 'the Great Offensive of 1335'.

two English earls, Hereford, who led the van, and, the last man on the roll (No. 277), the Earl of Warwick, Thomas de Beauchamp. This is borne out by the note that *l'autre conte et ses bachelers* (follow here). The Earl of Warwick is thus *l'autre conte*, for some reason not named until the end, and, if this is so, Nos. 32–52 will be his bachelors. This should be capable of verification from the nominal rolls in Cott. MS. Nero C viii. If this is not so, then the roll is a partial roll, of the muster at Newcastle.

As it stands the roll offers the following subdivisions: (i) Nos. 1–31 under Hereford, (ii) *l'autre conte* (Nos. 32–101), (iii) the king (No. 102) and the foreigners, leaving another 173 knights to make up the required 450 and form (iv) the knights who remained at Newcastle with Warenne.

The herald-painter of this roll, the man who *temp.* Henry VI turned the blazoned roll into a painted one, was not himself a very competent herald.[1] He has arranged his work as if he were a professional accountant whose hobby was heraldic painting, for he does not arrange his page as a scribe would in copying consecutive prose line by line, he works in columns like an exchequer clerk, i.e. the shields, if consecutive and related pairs, are, as they must be, taken into account:

1	4	and not		1	2
2	5	,,	,,	3	4
3	8	,,	,,	5	6

If the shields on the roll are to be numbered, this affects Nos. 2, 3, 4, 5 on every page.

[1] Herald painters first appear upon the records in 1347, when Stephen Doget stated that 45*s*. 4*d*. was due to him for painting 200 standards and 144 pennons of the [Black] Prince's arms, kept in his wardrobe at London (*B.P.R.* i. 47 of 16 Dec. 1347). Much later John Brown (d. 1532: see *D.N.B.* iii) was sergeant painter to Henry VIII, and painted shields, banners, and surcoats, etc., for tournaments, by patent of 1512. He was a member of the companies of Haberdashers and Painter Stainers, and had himself an elaborate coat of arms. He had a salary of £10 a year in 1527. It is noteworthy that no connection with the Heralds' College is mentioned.

OF EDWARD III'S REIGN, 1327–1377

As to the manuscript itself, foll. 122^v–123 of Fitz-William MS. 324 offer a blatant instance, of which there are many less horrid examples in the book, of coats of arms being 'transferred' in outline or even almost entire to the opposite page. The book must have been tightly bound when the colours were still moist or at an early date have been subjected to considerable pressure. In a reproduction in my possession this has given the appearance of over-painting, but that is not in question.

It could be suggested that the Carlisle Roll was painted for Humphrey de Bohun IX, the earl who died in 1336, as it begins with his arms. This would be in keeping with the cultivated tastes of the Bohun family in the fourteenth century. Seven fine manuscripts are associated with the Humphrey de Bohun who died in 1373, and with his aunt Eleanor.[1] He was a patron, too, of the poet John of Bridlington. He could have commissioned Cooke's Ordinary, a view that is made credible by the fact that the manuscript is found in Carmarthenshire in the fifteenth century. Some Marcher connection is clearly indicated, but no positive evidence of early ownership or provenance can be adduced.

The creation of Carlisle Herald has been assigned to 1327. There was, it is true, an affray either in that year or immediately before the Treaty of Northampton in 1328 with the Scots, but the whole episode has been described as a 'deep humiliation' for Edward III,[2] and I have not found that Edward 'passed near Carlisle' at this time.[3] What action there was took place at Stanhope Park in Northumberland and was no occasion for the creation of heralds, which in any case Edward could not have done on his own authority as he was still in tutelage and was only 14 or 15 years of age. Mortimer was occupied

---

[1] See *A Book about Books* (Murray, 2nd edn., 1948), 71–3.
[2] McKisack, *The Fourteenth Century*, 118. No date of place or time is given for the muster, but York was undoubtedly the base.
[3] Wagner, *Heralds and Heraldry* (2nd edn., 1956), 35, 37.

in dealing with pretenders to the throne and with arrangements for the murder of the deposed king, who had been conveniently removed to Berkeley Castle. Also the narrative of Froissart says explicitly that it was five years before April 1338, and this can hardly be stretched so far as 1327 by any method of reckoning. Finally, the chronicle speaks of an expedition of Edward III in Scotland, in as many words. In 1327 it was, on the contrary, a Scottish invasion of Northumberland.

About three weeks before the second Dunstable tournament Edward had been making merry at Newcastle-on-Tyne (Sunday, 19 June 1334), where Edward Balliol had come to do homage for the kingdom that he owed to Edward III's support. The Bruces had fled to France and Balliol was safe for a time. On the Sunday that he did homage for Scotland, the English king was attended by a herald-minstrel called Andrew Clarincell, and his companions,[1] who probably compiled the original of the Balliol Roll on this occasion. Since the matter is put in this way, it would seem that Andrew Clarenceux was the herald-minstrel king who compered the entertainment, perhaps a music-hall show with Andrew as the producer. Edward did not patronize the more advanced mystery plays, though he was a traditionalist and a lover of ritual. In some ways absurdly old-fashioned, he or his ministers attempted in 1353 a distraint of knighthood at the £15 level. This was the harshest ever, almost a panic measure. Conceivably it was made necessary by the ravages of the Black Death.[2] An income of that size in the mid fourteenth century would hardly have sufficed for a knight's armour, and certainly not for his horse. Unless he had made an unusually favourable contract with some great lord in advance, he would have had to mortgage his estates, as some English crusaders had done in the preceding cen-

---

[1] Wagner, *Heralds and Heraldry*, 159, from Brit. Mus. Add. MS. 46350 (a wardrobe account). The Annals of Oseney in *Ann. Mon.* iv. 349, give the date.
[2] I have seen no statistics on this point.

tury. Edward III's grandfather had treated such devoted knights with some generosity, and so did the Black Prince, but Edward himself had years of financial struggle before he could keep an army for long in the field.

It has been thought that Andrew's title was a creation of this date, and that it was revived for the Duke of Clarence's own creation in 1362. Clarence might seem an effeminate or perhaps Frenchified name for a duke, though Clarenceux is better. But the historical implications of the word are very great. It comes not from abroad but from the honour of Clare, a substantial part of which came to the Duke through his child-wife, Elizabeth de Burgh (she was rising four years old when they were married in 1343), who was the granddaughter of Elizabeth de Clare, the wealthy coheiress of the earldom of Gloucester as sister to the last earl, Gilbert de Clare. With Clarence in 1362 we are not here concerned, nor with his herald if he had one.[1] For the herald king, and Andrew Clarence, presumably took his name as herald of the Gloucester estates, with its family seat at Clare in Suffolk. All the great marcher earls had their private heralds, and, though there is as yet no record of a Clare Herald in the thirteenth century, we are I think entitled to assume one. It is not a big assumption. Gilbert de Clare died at Bannockburn in 1314, leaving three coheiresses and a terrible legacy of trouble to the whole kingdom. On the break-up of the Great Earldom of Gloucester in 1314, its herald would have to seek other employment. The sisters would have no use for him, and so it is thought that he, like many another private official in that period, took service with the Crown. If this theory is acceptable, we have found the missing Gloucester Herald. It will be remembered that the Clares themselves outranked the other

---

[1] The argument is that Lionel of Clarence and the herald both take their title from the Clare estates, but Clarenceux ante-dates Lionel, who was born 1338, the third son of Edward III, and began life as Lionel of Antwerp. McKisack (p. 267) is in error and Andrew did not take his title from him.

earls in land and wealth and political influence. In the mid thirteenth century Earl Gilbert the Red had answered for 400 knights' fees of his inheritance, as, besides the earldom of Gloucester and Hertford, he had the rich and highly privileged lands in Glamorgan and large estates in Ireland.

It was the support of Earl Gilbert, son of the earl poisoned by his estate agent Walter de Scoteny in 1262, who won for Simon de Montfort the battle of Lewes, and the loss of that support turned the scale at Evesham. From that time no one doubted that Gloucester was the most powerful man in the country next to the king. He nearly overthrew the government by a rash advance on London in 1267 to obtain better terms for the Disinherited, but once he had made his peace with Edward there was no longer fear of civil war. He should have gone on crusade in 1269, and did indeed take the cross; but he never went. He raised no trouble for the regency government during the Lord Edward's four years on crusade. Not only his wealth and personal history are important in this context. He owned the earliest recorded English seignorial coat of arms, the Clare chevronny coat, found as early as between 1141 and 1146.[1] Sir Anthony Wagner has on this cited J. H. Round's conclusion 'that the reign of Stephen was the period in which heraldic bearings were assuming a definite form', and himself concludes that it was at that time that they were probably introduced into England. Sir Anthony points also to King Stephen's well-known love of tournaments as significant in this connection.[2] The love of tournaments continued in the family, and in the mid thirteenth century they organized their own, which must have necessitated the presence of a herald. Richard de Clare was a fine lance. When his brother William in 1252 lost all his horses and arms at a tournament on the Continent, Richard came and won

---

[1] See Wagner, *Heralds and Heraldry*, 15.
[2] Ibid. 17.

them all back for him.[1] This love of adventure skipped a generation, for Gilbert the Red 'displayed no interest in tournaments or other social festivities on the Continent, and had little to do with the king's [foreign] relatives'.[2]

By tradition, wealth, and personal prestige the Earl of Gloucester needed a herald as much or more than any other marcher earl, at any date. Gilbert the Red was undoubtedly a member of the committee for regulating tournaments in 1267, but he had had enough serious fighting to do as a young man at Lewes and Evesham, quite apart from his campaigns against the Welsh, and his private war with Hereford. So he did not indulge in tournaments or pilgrimages, and he got rid of his Lusignan child-bride as expeditiously as he could. The last Earl Gilbert reverted to type. He is not mentioned at the fateful Wallingford tournament of December 1307, but was one of the earls whose retinue is known at the Dunstable tournament of 1310. He and other magnates received three writs in August and September 1313 forbidding them to tourney. There was a steady flow of such prohibitions, individual and general, to within four months of the battle of Bannockburn, and they start again in 1317.

These earls quite clearly needed a herald, and it is therefore suggested that Andrew de Clarentia or Clarenceux was in fact the last of a line of anonymous heralds. Few other private heralds have left their mark before 1334, but it cannot be doubted that they were there. As Clarenceux, Andrew had the southern province, thus including the Clare estates, but as a royal herald in or after 1334 he became (I suppose) Andrew Rex Norroy,[3] unless both northern and southern provinces were at that date served by Andrew, which seems most improbable.

[1] *Ann. Theok.* 151, 152.
[2] Michael Altschul, *The Clare Family*, (1217–1314), 102.
[3] In 1338 Andrew Norroy is found, and in 1348 Andrew Norray is still making minstrelsy before the king (Wagner, *Heralds and Heraldry*, 27). If born *c.* 1290 he could be 57 as Norroy and 24 as the dashing young Earl's herald—a pure supposition—at Bannockburn.

The Balliol Roll

This presents two problems: the date of the compilation of the list of Scottish knights which it comprised, and secondly the date of the painted roll at the end of whose dorse it is found. The list of names has been ascribed to 1332, the year of Edward Balliol's coronation as King of Scotland. This in itself is not a satisfactory reason, for knights did not appear in battle array at coronations, though heralds were present, as at the opening of Parliament and other ceremonies. It is, at this period certainly, not a fitting occasion, as a battle siege or tournament was, for the compilation of such a record. The roll, though it relates to Scotland, is of English provenance. It could be a roll of homages made when these were done at Berwick in 1334, the year after Edward III had won the battle of Halidon Hill near by, on 19 July 1333. If this is so the roll as we have it is not the original, for it has been painted on the lower part of the dorse of Cooke's Ordinary, which cannot, since it includes the Earls of Northampton (William de Bohun, created 1337)[1] and Salisbury (William de Montacute, created 1337), have been painted before 1337. There seems to be no reason for not accepting this copy of the Balliol Roll as an addition made about 1338–9 to an existing roll.

Logically the roll could be of any date after 1337, but it is unlikely that a roll of Scottish followers of a puppet king, as Edward Balliol was, would have been made after he had ceased to play any active part in the retention of his dignity. In spite of Halidon Hill, and in spite of successive annual invasions of Scotland by his overlord in 1334–7, Balliol never established himself as king. In the autumn of 1337 Edward III went to war with France, and Balliol left Scotland at the end of 1338. No English

---

[1] Not Huntingdon. See *C.E.M.R.A.* 54. The Balliol Roll is not the oldest list of Scottish coats. This distinction belongs to the Ragman Roll, and its seals, described by Sir James Ramsay as the 'Ur-Armorial of the Scottish gentry'.

herald would have thought it worth while to make a list of his supporters after that date.

Cotgrave and Cooke

The two Ordinaries, or collection of coats classified by charge, known as Cotgrave's Ordinary and Cooke's Ordinary have much in common. The former has been printed,[1] but Cooke's Ordinary, now in the possession of Sir Anthony Wagner, has not. Cotgrave will here be considered first, because it is the shorter manuscript and could well have preceded and acted as a model for Cooke's work. There is nothing whatever to suggest that Cooke preceded Cotgrave. Unfortunately, while the original of Cooke is extant, Cotgrave depends upon a sixteenth-century copy of a blazoned original made about 1340.[2]

So far as the provenance of these two rolls is concerned, the field for conjecture is wide open, and, so far as I know, no one has suggested a possible origin for either manuscript. The most obvious solution would be that they, having so much in common, were made one for the Constable and one for the Marshal at the outbreak of the Hundred Years War, but this is almost certainly not so; though two such rolls are precisely the kind of record that would be necessary for the proper functioning of the *Curia Militaris*, which is first seen in action as a properly constituted court at the siege of Calais in 1346. But there is no Bohun (born 1309), Earl of Essex and Constable of England, 1336–61, on Cotgrave's Roll, and, though as

[1] Sir Harris Nicholas (ed.), *A Roll of Arms Compiled in the Reign of Edward III, 1337–40* (London, William Pickering, 1829). Sir Anthony Wagner very kindly confirmed for me that Bohun, the Constable from 1336, is not on Cotgrave's Roll.

[2] *C.E.M.R.A.* 60. Cotgrave depends on the College of Arms MS. (used by Nicolas) made in 1562 for Mr. Hugh FitzWilliam of Sprotsbrough, Lincs., by Hugh Cotgrave of Sermes, who found it hard to read. In 1562 Mr. Hugh FitzWilliam, who also had the Dering Roll, possessed the original now lost. Lincoln is right off the eighteenth-century stage-coach map and the manuscripts might well have lain there for centuries before 1562.

a marcher earl he is a candidate for the authorship of Cooke's Ordinary at Carmarthen, there turns out to be no substance in this hypothesis.[1]

England is rich in Ordinaries of arms,

[in which] designs of one type, as coats with lions or coats with chevrons, are grouped together. The chief use of such a work would be for identification. Such a practical working tool would almost necessarily be the work of a professional. While the whole continent of Europe can apparently show no single medieval Ordinary, in England we have Cooke's and Cotgrave's of Edward III's reign, William Jenyns's of Richard II's, and the great painted and blazoned collection which goes by the name of Thomas Jenyns little if at all later. The still extant painted original of Cooke's Ordinary may be regarded as the father of all its kind.[2]

There is more knowledge than I possess in this excellent passage but I take leave to doubt the question of paternity.

In my view Cotgrave's Ordinary and not Cooke's was the Ur-Ordinary and its author is therefore to be regarded as an even greater innovator than the man who inspired the P.R.A.'s arrangement by counties. The latter system would be, however, of greater immediate value for the government in time of peace. Rolls of this kind were new because they classified the charges in an orderly fashion, but Cotgrave does more than this; he places an earl at the head of each section, where possible, thus: Suffolk, crosses; Arundel, lions; Monthermer, eagles; Tyes, chevrons; Gloucester, chevronels; Audley, frets; Montague Earl of Salisbury, chiefs; Oxford, quarterly; Derby, lions passant; Angus, conquefoils and roses.

This could be a contemporary adaptation of Cooke's Ordinary, but historically speaking this is unlikely. Cooke's Ordinary is much the longer—644 plus two painted shields as against 556 blazoned shields with 219

---

[1] Not only Bohun but Warwick is missing from Cotgrave. Bohun should be about No. 310 and Warwick about No. 250.

[2] *C.E.M.R.A.* 15, ll. 9–19.

illustrations in the margin. The comparison is hard to make because Cooke is an original of about 1340 and Cotgrave a sixteenth-century copy which omits many baptismal names and corrupts many surnames.

A closer look at the way in which Cotgrave is arranged shows that, although there are five plain crosses on the Carlisle Roll of 1335, there are no plain crosses in Cotgrave. The roll starts with the newly created Earl of Suffolk, Robert Ufford, who bore a cross engrailed.[1] Other kinds of crosses follow, paté or florettée. Crosses were not the earliest form of charges, but they became very common. It seems likely that Cotgrave begins with engrailed crosses because the Earl of Suffolk bore one, or in other words that the roll was made for Robert Ufford on his creation as earl in 1337. There would seem to be no reason for this procedure unless Suffolk was the herald's patron. Suffolk had, indeed, been close to the court, and as a king's knight he had been steward of the royal household in 1336, though only for three weeks.

It may be that the author of Cotgrave was a man of considerable powers of invention, and that the idea of an Ordinary was his own. The theologians had their 'distinctions' and the heralds their 'differences'. But it needs a far greater mental effort, and a more far-reaching mind, to note and classify essential similarities. As has been pointed out, heralds at this date did not even make indexes, and, when they did in Tudor times, idiosyncrasies of spelling made indexes by vowels after the initial letter (as used and possibly invented by Dugdale in his *Monasticon*) the only useful method. Collection is a primitive urge but few people have analytical minds. The urge to classify came to the heralds when the government moved north to York for six years, and any inquiring mind perceived a number of new specimens, and thought that they would look better if arranged in patterns. At first no great originality was needed, but to develop a logical

[1] From this time often called *recercelée* instead of engrailed.

system, as Cotgrave did, required a powerful mind. Like all discoveries it is fundamentally simple, but heraldry had existed for two hundred years before it was attempted.

If this is so, the College of Arms owes much to the anonymous author of Cotgrave. He was a fourteenth-century genealogist, interested in tracing the relationship between the owners of similar coats of arms, much as John Horace Round did. This leaps to the eye in the earlier sections of his work, where family or tenurial relationships are clearly demonstrated. The terminology of the blazon is often clumsy, but it might well be a draft or a first version for Cooke.

Cotgrave's Ordinary is thus not simply a classified list of coats of arms: it is a list of great men and their kinsfolk. The intention, I believe, was to show to what clan or family group a man belonged. From the purely historical point of view these two Ordinaries are an important heraldic development, part of the upsurge of fourteenth-century chivalry associated with the great military triumphs of Edward III at Sluys, Crécy, and Poitiers, the Round Tables at Windsor, and the foundation of the Order of the Garter.

Cooke's Ordinary

The first extant *original* Ordinary in England and therefore in Europe (for no medieval continental Ordinaries are known to exist) is that associated with the name of Cooke.[1] The original of Cotgrave's Ordinary was very close to this in arrangement and content, but it may be thought that, if that original existed, it could claim priority. Cotgrave is, if anything, rather before 1340, and Cooke quite probably before 1342.

The original manuscript of Cooke's roll is in the possession of Sir Anthony Wagner, the owner also of the Dering Roll and other important rolls as recorded in his *Catalogue*,

[1] *C.E.M.R.A.* xv.

where the Ordinary is fully described and illustrated in colour.[1]

This Ordinary is endorsed on the last five membranes with the Balliol Roll. The history of its migration is mysterious and fascinating. About 1430 it was sent to the sheriff's office in Carmarthen for repairs, which were made with the aid of old and surplus fifteenth-century subsidiary documents of the Welsh county court (cf. the Boroughbridge Roll with its writs from a sheriff's office on the face of the roll). So Sir Rhys Ap Thomas, the Welsh High Sheriff at that time, was probably already the owner, and a later Sir Rhys Ap Thomas (1449–1525), a Welsh gentleman at the Tudor court, proposed to give or bequeath it to the Franciscans of Carmarthen.

The roll itself contains nothing to show a special interest in Wales. The Welsh connection may be fortuitous and misleading. As the roll was repaired with a portion of an account roll of Sir Rhys Ap Thomas as sheriff, it could have passed from him to his namesake, a Knight of the Garter, who lived from 1449 to 1525. The book passed from him to the Grey Friars of Carmarthen a few years after the death of Sir Rhys.[2]

The Ordinary is an English roll ascribed to about 1340 and endorsed with the Balliol Roll made (or copied from one that was made) in Scotland in 1334. Further, this Ordinary, when it was fully legible, used to begin, as is known from early copies, 'Kelkfeld de Escoce'. As with some other rolls the secret seems to be given away at the

---

[1] Ibid., 58–9 and Plate V. It passed from Grey Friars to Sir Robert Cooke, Clarenceux (1576), and was later owned by Sir Thomas Phillipps, Bart. (d. 1872).

[2] See the *Dictionary of Welsh Biography*. The English edition is said by Welsh authorities to be better than the Welsh edition. This Sir Rhys was associated with the Tudor revival of interest in the tournament. It will be remembered that Henry VIII was himself a considerable jouster. It was therefore quite natural for Sir Rhys to hold a great tournament, to which he invited all the leading men in Wales, to celebrate his creation as K.G. From every point of view he was favourably placed to have dealings with heralds, and his activities as a knight could explain his interest in rolls of arms.

top. It seems that we must trace some connection between Carmarthen and Scotland and the Balliol Roll. This can be found in the person of Henry of Lancaster, called Henry of Grosmont, created Earl of Derby in 1337, and Duke of Lancaster in 1351. He had inherited an interest in South Wales, and his father's grant to him of the family lands there (1334) included Kidwelly and Monmouth. The excellent account of this colourful man in the *Dictionary of National Biography* fails to mention that in 1342 he was granted the castle town and county of Carmarthen as keeper for ten years.[1] Thus, at the time when the roll could have been made, we have a keeper of the shire and castle who had all the qualifications that would be expected in an owner of this roll, for he had fought in numerous Scottish campaigns and was a great tournament man and jouster. On 10 October 1341 when he was at Roxburghe, he was appointed captain-general of the army against the Scots. In December a six-month truce was made and Derby took the opportunity to indulge in his favourite sport. He vanquished Sir William Douglas of Liddesdale in a tilt at Roxburghe, and persuaded Sir Alexander Ramsay of Dalhousie to joust with with him in a twenty-a-side match. On 3 April 1342 he was appointed to arrange another truce and in October he went to Britanny with the king. He could between these dates have taken seisin in person of his recent grant of Carmarthen, but it is more likely that he left the matter to his steward, or perhaps a herald, who would work with one of his agents already looking after the family estates near by. In the spring of 1343 he went on a mission to Avignon and then to Castille, and while there fought the Moors at Algeciras. On his return to England he again went north to negotiate with the Scots. At the great Windsor tournament in 1344 he acted for his father as Steward of England. Derby became Lancaster next year on the death of his father, who at the age of 48 was old

[1] *Cal. F.R.* (1333–47), 263–4 (17 Feb. 1342).

and blind, and had taken no part in affairs for the last fifteen years. Henry inherited the Savoy from his father and rebuilt it at a cost of 52,000 marks which he had picked up in French ransoms in the 1345 campaign. The rest of his public career, which was one great distinction in the French wars, need not concern us. Henry has been described as 'brave, courteous, charitable, just; and at once magnificent and personally temperate in his habits . . . he was loved and trusted by Edward III beyond any other of his lords'.[1] The more one reads of this family in the thirteenth and fourteenth centuries, the sadder one feels about the shocking ineptitude and folly of Earl Thomas.

It would be pleasant to think that Henry of Lancaster paid a flying visit to Carmarthen in 1342, but there is nothing to indicate this. The Welsh and the Marchers would have appreciated a little pomp and circumstance, as the king's officials had noticed when in 1302 they took seisin of the Bohun inheritance.[2] Henry of Lancaster was probably content, like Walter Mauny in Merionethshire, to be an absentee landlord. Cooke's Ordinary, however, which I suspect was made for Henry of Lancaster, could well have been taken there by the herald who made it, and left by accident or design in the castle, where it lay neglected until eventually repaired in the sheriff's office there. The herald could have borrowed Ufford's roll (Cotgrave) and improved upon it. This is to be taken as guesswork, inspired or otherwise. But it seems to me that the roll would not have been repaired in the sheriff's office in the castle unless it was already in an adjacent or nearby office. The owner would naturally take his roll for repair to the nearest record depository, or it could have been already there for safe-keeping. This is perhaps as near as we can get at the moment.

Along the Welsh March the greater English earldoms long retained their old fighting-grounds. Those of the

[1] T. F. Tout in *D.N.B.*   [2] *Cal. Misc. Inq.* ii, No. 1870.

lords of Lancaster were at Monmouth and Kidwelly; and the possession of Kidwelly took them as suitors to Carmarthen county court. And so it is thought that not Hereford nor Mauny nor the Black Prince but Henry of Grosmont (later Duke of Lancaster) had this roll made when he was Earl of Derby, and that his herald took it to Carmarthen Castle. The pedigree has often caused confusion:

```
                    Edmund of Lancaster
                            |
         _____|_____
        |                                       |
  Thomas (Steward),   Henry (Steward), d. 1345, after pottering about
  executed 1322.      for 15 years doing good works.
                            |
                      Henry of Grosmont (Steward), d. 1365. A Marcher
                      in S. Wales from 1334.[1] Earl of Derby 1337, Earl of
                      Lancaster 1345, Duke 1351.
```

Powell's Roll, c. *1350*

In great contrast to the two famous Ordinaries is the almost contemporary Powell's Roll compiled about 1350. This is an old-fashioned piece of work,[2] reminiscent of Camden's Roll of *c.* 1280 or Collins's of *c.* 1296. The roll, a painted one, of 669 shields begins with the king, his son, some earls, followed by a confused list of knights and barons (or *chivalers* and lords), and occasionally another earl (No. 418: Warwick; No. 545: Warwick, Leicester, Winchester, Ulster, and Valence). Some of the persons named are contemporary, others long dead (e.g. Adam Bannister). Some (as Botetourt) occur twice, with correct arms, but hopelessly corrupt spelling of names; signifying either two generations of the same family, or simply that the compiler had come across a fresh source and in his agglomerative fashion had simply tacked it on to his

[1] See D. L. Evans in *The History of Carmarthenshire*, ed. J. E. Lloyd (Cardiff, 1935), vol. i: *The Later Middle Ages* (1282–1536), 201–67, especially 210.
[2] Edited by J. Greenstreet in Jewitt's *Reliquary* (N.S.), vols. iii (1889) and iv (1890) from Bod. Lib. MS. Ashmole 804, 1–28. These articles have been reproduced in facsimile and elaborately edited (1963) for the Society of Genealogists by Prof. R. C. Gale.

existing stock-in-trade.[1] Such a list would be of little practical use to a herald or genealogist unless he learned it by heart.

This roll (Bod. Lib. MS. Ashmole 804 ff. 1–28, a vellum book with painted leaves) is of considerable interest and yields at least some of its secrets upon a close inspection. For if we work through it name by name, attaching counties where possible to the names, it reveals itself as a roll with a strong East Anglian bias. It is composite, and the second part is the earlier, for it is noticeable that families whose arms are repeated bear the simpler version in the second part, i.e. it is a generation or so earlier, and contains names of thirteenth-century knights like Peter de Montfort of Beaudesert (No. 420).

There are seven Uffords on the roll, and a large group of East Anglian knights. Sir Robert Ufford, who became the first Earl of Suffolk in 1337, had large fiefs in Suffolk, Norfolk, Lincolnshire, and London. His grandfather Robert de Ufford (d. 1298), a crusader with Edward I, founded the greatness of the family. He was a younger son of John de Peyton, and took the name Ufford from his lordship of Ufford in Suffolk. The man who became first Earl of Suffolk (1298–1369) was the second, but eldest surviving, son of Robert de Ufford (1279–1316) and his wife Cecily de Valognes. His estates were increased in 1330 by a grant of the castle and town of Orford in Suffolk for life, the manor of Gravesend in Kent, and Costessy and Burgh in Norfolk. He was associated with William de Montague in the attack on Mortimer at Nottingham Castle, and was rewarded with the manors of Causton and Fakenham in Norfolk and houses in Cripplegate that had lately belonged to John Maltravers. He was summoned to Parliament as a baron from January 1332. No other family is so well represented on the roll.

[1] In this method, or lack of it, Powell's Roll is strongly reminiscent of Collins's Roll of 1296 (see *History and Heraldry*, 96–101) and in both instances it is extremely difficult to follow the compiler.

Suffolk was very much a king's knight, serving for a time as warden of Bothwell Castle, south of Glasgow, as a justice of the forest, and as keeper of the forests south of the Trent (1331). He acquired great diplomatic experience and like his predecessors was a great tournament man: he was at Dunstable in 1342 and at the great jousts in London. He was also at the Round Table at Windsor in February 1344 and at the September tournament at Hertford. He was an early, though not a founder, member of the Order of the Garter, and he was strenuous in arms at Crécy and Poitiers—just the man in fact to need a herald and want a roll of arms.[1] The roll which I associate with his name was probably made in a hurry, by a skilled herald. It could have been done while he was at home as commissioner of array, though no addition seems to have been made after about 1350. Such a roll of nearly 700 painted shields must have been preceded by a draft, even if other rolls were at hand.[1]

[1] There is a good account in *D.N.B.* For the tournaments see Mur. 159, 232, and for the arms P.R.A. (Suffolk), 471–2, Dering, and Collins 126, *sable, a cross engrailed or.*

V

PRIVATE ADMINISTRATION: THE HONOUR OF WALLINGFORD

THIS chapter is not in any way exciting, but it will serve as a brief reminder that the country gentry of the fourteenth century were rarely gentlemen of leisure, as they could be in a later age. It is likely, indeed, that no section of the community worked harder than they did, and much of their work in time of peace must have been grindingly dull.

The survival of contemporary records makes Wallingford a convenient example of the working of a great honour in the fourteenth century. It may serve, too, as a link with what has been said elsewhere of the estates of Richard of Cornwall,[1] who held it from 1231 until he died in 1272. Under Edmund of Cornwall (d. 1300)[2] and the Black Prince[3] the administration of the honour can be clearly seen, but the immediate purpose of this chapter is to illustrate the part played by the country gentry in the peaceful service of the magnates, as stewards, feodaries, councillors, and estate agents, or as judges under the king.

The honour was always close to the Crown, and so was highly privileged,[4] and to that extent its component honours and baronies are not typical of smaller independent baronies. It did not lose its identity in 1337 when the

[1] Denholm-Young, *Richard of Cornwall* (1947), 164.
[2] Miss Midgley's edition of the few surviving estate accounts is of much value (Camden Soc. 1942, 1945). On Edmund's death Wallingford was granted in turn to Piers Gaveston, Hugh Despenser, and Queen Isabella.
[3] *B.P.R.*
[4] In 1285 Edmund, who seems to have inherited his father's acquisitive habits, claimed exemption from *quo warranto* inquiries (*Cal. Chancery Warrants*, 25. Twelve unspecified writs are mentioned).

Cornwall was erected into a duchy. From 1231, when Henry III granted it with the manor of Watlington (Oxfordshire) to his brother Richard of Cornwall, Wallingford was held for three fees, though it consisted of 120, of which twenty-seven and a quarter lay in Oxfordshire.[1] Most of these fees owed suit to the court of the honour at Wallingford. They formed a compact group in the south of the county, including the four and a half Chiltern hundreds. The connection with Berkshire, which had the same sheriff, was very close.[2]

When the Duchy of Cornwall was created in 1337, this highly privileged liberty, with hundredal jurisdiction and return of writs, thus excluding the sheriff, was administered, as it had been since 1231, with the honour of St. Valery and other Oxfordshire manors formerly held by Richard of Cornwall. In 1212 this unit comprised, besides the main manors, about a quarter, and later all, of the fees in Oxfordshire.[3] The honour was diminished by Edmund's grants to his father's Cistercian foundation at Hailes, his own abbey at Rewley, and his college of Bonhommes at Ashridge.[4]

By the fourteenth century the honour was left with no demesne manors, but the bailiwick of Wallingford included the important manors of Watlington, Bensington,

---

[1] The history of the individual fees up to 1300 is given by H. E. Salter, *The Boarstall Chartulary* (O.H.S. 1930). As for the earlier history, Wigod, lord of the honour in 1066, was sheriff of Oxford and a supporter of the Conqueror. He gave his daughter in marriage to Robert d'Oilly and their daughter Matilda married Miles Crispin, who already held the manors of the honour. On his death without issue in 1107 Matilda's second husband Brian FitzCount succeeded him. Much later they surrendered their lands and entered religion. After its seizure by Henry II (c. 1154) Wallingford was held by the Crown till 1189, when Richard I gave it to his brother John. It reverted to the Crown on John's rebellion in 1194.

[2] *V.C.H. Oxon.* i. 389.

[3] *Book of Fees*, i. 102–3. The service due from the barony of St. Valery was at least five times between 1201 and 1268 regarded as ten knights (Ault, *Private Jurisdiction*, 178–9).

[4] Midgley, pp. xii–xiv, 148. Edmund gave the manor of Asthall to his half-brother, Richard of Cornwall (ibid. xxi).

THE HONOUR OF WALLINGFORD 123

and Henley with the borough. The honour court of St. Valery is first seen in action in a deed of between 1172 and 1189, when Bernard of St. Valery sued a tenant in his own court at North Oseney, outside Oxford.[1] It next comes into view in 1272–3[2] and in 1296–7. As with the court of the honour of Wallingford, worth about £8 a year at this period, there is at first sight the appearance of considerable activity, but the profits were made up largely of fines for the relaxation of suit, which seem to have varied according to the importance of the tenant. The suitors included the Abbot of Oseney, the Priors of St. Frideswide, Oxford, Brackley, and Bitlesden, the Master of the Temple, and all the military tenants. Though the view of frankpledge was kept quite distinct, it is impossible to separate the purely honorial aspect from its function as a manorial court.

The manorial account rolls present a curiously static picture. There is no mention of the Earl of Cornwall or his friends or officials staying at the demesne manors, though their apartments were kept in repair. There is no mention of view or audit, or any attempt to estimate profits, but enough is said for us to be certain that when Edmund succeeded to the earldom he at once changed the system. Active conciliar control is seen under him, but the names of the councillors, apart from the Treasurer and Wardrober, remain unknown.

The profits of the honour court of St. Valery were of the order of £35, largely for fines in connection with the frankpledge system, though practically nothing is heard of its ultimate purposes—the keeping of the king's peace. The annual value of the honour to the Earl, before it was diminished by the loss of Ambrosden, Asthall, Yarnton, and North Oseney, approached £500, but the surplus would not usually be more than £300 a year.[3]

[1] MS. Magd. Coll., Oxon., charter No. 631 (Woodstock 9).
[2] P.R.O. Min. Acct. 961/6 and 958/19.
[3] Cf. P.R.O. Min. Acct. 958/19 (undated).

The honour of St. Valery was administered by a steward, usually the steward of the honour of Wallingford, and it was he, not the bailiff or reeve, who rendered a composite account for each manor in his bailiwick. Estate agents of this calibre were usually country gentry.

The system of account common to all the estates of the earldom of Cornwall was changed between 1270 and 1272, presumably on the accession of Earl Edmund, and the change from Wallingford to Berkhamsted as the financial and administrative centre of the earldom. Continuity was provided by the continued activity of Michael of Northampton as one of the Earl's wardrobers in 1272–3.[1] He had been one of Earl Richard's executors, and acted as his attorney when Earl Edmund went overseas in 1280.[2] A mode of account was introduced more logical and rigid than that found on the other great agglomerations of estates known to us, that is the Fortibus estates or those of Roger Bigod, the Earl Marshal,[3] in that the foreign expenses and *liberaciones* are excluded from the body of the account. They are now added at the end, after the total indebtedness of the steward to the auditors has been declared, and they are added in a different hand—presumably that of the auditor's clerk at the audit.[4] There is increased centralization and increased conciliar control.[5] The new system was meant to ensure that receipts and expenses would fluctuate far less from year to year, minor fluctuations could be more easily checked, and, if necessary, farming profits could be (and probably were) estimated.

---

[1] Cf. P.R.O. Min. Acct. 958/19 (undated).   [2] Midgley, p. xxxiii.
[3] For these see my *Seignorial Administration in England* (Oxford, 1937).
[4] In 1272–3 a surviving account roll (P.R.O. Min. Acct. 961/6) shows that the sum of all debts was £482. 15s. 11d., but the steward must have had a large cash reserve (relating to this honour?) not shown in the account, for he paid out a total of £650, thus producing £167. 4s. 1d. 'out of the blue' or from his reserves at Wallingford. About £350 was paid into the Earl's wardrobe through Sir Michael of Northampton, one of Earl Richard's executors, and 'dominus Paganus'.
[5] *Richard of Cornwall*, 162–3.

The Black Prince's apanage was on an even larger scale than that of Earl Richard or Earl Edmund. It included Cornwall, Wallingford, St. Valery, and Berkhamsted, as well as Wales and Chester, and the Duchy of Aquitaine, though this was now reduced to a strip of coast. These scattered estates needed a highly organized system of local administration, with central offices comprising Exchequer, Wardrobe, and Council at Westminster. So the Oxfordshire estates now accounted not at Wallingford or Berkhamsted but at Westminster. From the first volume of the existing register, the work of the chief local and central officials can be seen.

At the top there was a steward and surveyor for all the Prince's lands; this man was also a justice and a member of his council. There was also a feodary for all the estates. For the Thames Valley estates of Wallingford and St. Valery, and for Berkhamsted, the Prince had an escheator, Thomas Gervays of Wycombe, his yeoman,[1] who also collected the moneys arising from the greenwax and due at the royal exchequer. With the Black Prince's accession to the Thames Valley estates the administrative centre of these honours was now at Westminster, where the first Duke established his Exchequer, Wardrobe, and Council. The only permanent demesne manors in Oxfordshire were Beckley and Watlington. An occasional manor such as Ipsden (William Basset had been tenant) or Whitchurch escheated to him. The Oxfordshire manor of Bensington was farmed to the tenants for £19. 11s. 5½d. 'from time out of mind', which really means by charter of Earl Richard of Cornwall to the twenty-five tenants in common, not in severalty.[2] Beckley, too, was farmed, except the park, to Tideman de Limbergh.[3]

In 1351 Sir Bartholomew de Burgherssh the son, in succession to Sir Ralph Spigurnell, took at farm for

[1] B.P.R. i (Index).
[2] Ibid. iv. 7–8 (A.D. 1351), 42. The tenants also owed £80 a year for the town (ibid. 44). [3] Ibid. 32–3.

twelve years at £200 a year the stewardship of the town and honour of Wallingford, the honour of St. Valery, the four and a half Chiltern hundreds, and the Constableship of the castle. The bargain included rents, services, suits, perquisites of the view of frankpledge, chattels of felons and fugitives, but not knights' fees, advowsons, escheats, wardships, and marriages.[1] The Prince had a strong, highly centralized, and unscrupulous administration which attracted and enforced suit to the honour court of Wallingford or to the hundred court of the four and a half hundreds at Benson, where it was not due; as again from the tenants of the manor and hundreds of Bampton, which belonged to the Earl of Pembroke. The age of bailiff-farming had passed, and most of the demesnes were farmed out, saving only parks, studs, and fisheries, e.g. the oak-woods at Beckley and the beeches at Berkhamsted. Now it was the feodary who was the important man to look after the feudal dues and advowsons, matters that in the age of bailiff-farming had fallen to the lot of the bailiffs and stewards, except where there was no demesne. We can see this by a study of the Fortibus estates. There was an unmistakable tendency for the Prince's ministers to encroach upon other jurisdictions. Examples are seen at Crowmarsh Giffard and the Earl of Pembroke's manor and hundred of Bampton, in favour of the honour court at Wallingford, or in the court for the four and a half Chiltern hundreds at Benson, or in the Bampton portion of the Aumale manor of Whitchurch.[2] A similar tendency is observable in general for royal justices to encroach upon private jurisdictions. Until about 1300 it had often been the other way round, but in spite of periodical set-backs the tide continued to flow in favour of the Crown.

The multiple duties of the feodaries are set out in a commission of 1361 to Richard de Stratton, appointed to

[1] Worth only a few shillings, cf. *B.P.R.* iv. 3.
[2] Ibid. 52.

THE HONOUR OF WALLINGFORD 127

act in Oxfordshire and eight other counties.[1] There were two other feodaries covering the other fifteen English counties in which the Prince had fees. Stratton was given full powers to seize property and distrain for dues. He had to claim and collect the profits before justices in eyre and of assize, or justices of the forest and of inquests, all manner of fines, issues, ransoms, amercements, chattels, forfeitures, escheats, voidances; year, day and waste, murder fines, chattels of felons and fugitives, together with the moneys of the greenwax, answering at the Prince's Exchequer at Westminster. For all this he received £5 a year. Returns of writs and all manner of executions were omitted because Burgherssh had them as part of his farm of Wallingford. The commissions to the three feodaries provide a comprehensive enumeration, though hardly a philosophical definition of the various facets of feudalism.

The Prince's administration worked very closely with— and indeed, interlocked with—that of the king. The feodary was the Prince's escheator. 'Mr. John Alverton, the steward of the lands of the chamber [in Oxfordshire], was at the same time lieutenant of the Prince's steward of Wallingford and St. Valery and was frequently employed by both Prince and King in Bucks. and neighbouring counties',[2] for example as escheator of Oxfordshire.[3] Under John of Gaunt the grouping of counties tended to vary: in 1380 John Wolf was feodary in Oxfordshire, Dorset, Hampshire, and Wiltshire; other groupings are known.[4] The relationship between the two systems was very close, for the Prince was allowed, as the Countess Isabella had been before him, to use the machinery of the Exchequer to collect his debts—hence the mention of 'issues of the green wax' in the feodary's commission.

The demesnes continued to be diminished by grants for

[1] Ibid. 374–5.
[2] Tout, *Chapters*, vol. v, Chap. XVIII, § II, 359.
[3] *C.P.R.* (1350–4), 497.
[4] John of Gaunt's *Register* (Camden Soc. i (1911), ii (1933)), Nos. 189, 198, 817.

life, or for a term of years,[1] and, after 1356, by lavish rewards in return for good services at Poitiers, for after the battle the lands granted out by the Prince would, had they all been granted to one man, have sustained him in modest comfort as an earl.[2] The administration, though greedy,[3] tried to be impartial, though Oxfordshire men played hardly any part in the Prince's entourage or in the administration of the English estates.[4]

Though the beginnings of conciliar activity are evident in the account rolls of Earl Edmund, the Council, now permanently at London, comes fully to light only under the Black Prince. It is continuously active and always ready to interfere in purely local matters. The judges Stonor and Shareshull were members. A large number of persons, great and small, were summoned before it, sometimes at great inconvenience to them. With the Bishop of Lincoln the Prince was on friendly terms, and the Bishop appointed him keeper of all his parks and warrens in England. The Bishop then sued tenants of the honour of Wallingford who were refusing to pay toll at his market at Thame. Then there was a dispute over common pasture between Dorchester and Warborough. The matter was eventually settled to the Bishop's satisfaction, but he had to remain in London specially for the purpose and of

[1] Whitchurch, Oxon., for 11 years (*B.P.R.* iv. 138).

[2] In 1355 Sir Roger de Cotesford took Watlington, at that time the only demesne manor of the honour of Wallingford, for life (ibid. 123); Sir John Chandos had a term in the manor of Beccles; Sir James Audley of Stratton Audley, a member of the Prince's household, was granted £400 a year for life out of the issue of Cornwall (ibid. 291).

[3] The three-weekly court of St. Valery at North Oseney continued to flourish, and as heretofore tried to extend its jurisdiction over the tenants of Beckley (*B.P.R.* iv. 209). In 1358 Burgherssh was ordered to take into hand all the bailiwicks of the honour of Wallingford that had been granted in fee, in consequence of many complaints about oppression and extortion, and to make suitable payment in compensation (ibid. 244). In pursuance of this order Sir William de Stratton, a bachelor of the Prince, lost his bailiwicks (ibid. 380).

[4] But Sir Edmund de Bereford (Barford St. Michael) was one of the Prince's trusted clerks. His three sisters, Agnes, Joan, and Margaret, married respectively Sir John Mautravers, Sir Gilbert de Elsefield, and Sir James Audley.

THE HONOUR OF WALLINGFORD

this he complained.¹ Again a Warborough tenant's sheep were impounded by the feodary in Wallingford Castle, where, as he said, they were without pasture and on the point of starving to death. To persuade the council to order the feodary to have them pastured, the tenant had to appear in London before it.² This is a small case concerning $5\frac{1}{2}$-marks-worth of felons' goods. Only these two instances are given, but there are hundreds of similar cases which could easily have been decided in a local court, at most the honour of Wallingford, instead of being summoned to London.³ A study of the whole apanage from this point of view would illuminate the motive behind the statute of Richard II against baronial councils.⁴

The early fourteenth century was a period when county families were being founded by professional lawyers: two examples are the Stonors of Stonor near Dorchester and the family of Shareshull in the north of Oxfordshire. Sir William Stonor, who flourished in the mid fifteenth century, and his family for four generations after their founder Sir John (d. 1354), had land in six counties.⁵ In each generation there were sheriffs, M.P.s, and J.P.s. But when a Stonor or a Shareshull became Chief Justice he left the circle of those who ran the shire and joined the ranks of those who pursued their fortunes in either the High Court or the domestic court of the king. 'It is curious', as Mr. Kingsford has remarked, 'that in a family of such fortune there was hardly one who did any real military service.'⁶ They form a striking contrast to the Scropes.

---

[1] *B.P.R.* iv. 277, 282, 292, 298, 348. [2] Ibid. 303, 306.
[3] It may be that the manor of Bensington, which had belonged to Earl Richard of Cornwall, was now regarded as within the honour of Wallingford, of which in fact it was never a constituent part (ibid. 448).
[4] Ibid. 148.
[5] The Stonor arms are *azure two annelets or a chief or*, as in Ashm. Roll 15A, No. 152.
[6] C. L. Kingsford (ed.), *The Stonor Papers* (Camden Soc., 4th Ser., 1919–20), vol. i, p. xxxix. No. 52 is an account rendered by John Coventre, under-sheriff for Oxon. and Berks. in 1427–8, a type of document that is rare indeed for an

Chief Justice Shareshull has in recent years been the subject of a detailed study.¹ Shareshull, who spelt his name in at least 107 different ways, married into the Purcell family shortly after 1316. He became serjeant-at-law in 1321 or 1322 and acquired land between the Cherwell and the Evenlode and later in Stanton Harcourt. He was promoted knight banneret when he became Chief Justice of Common Pleas in 1333, but the unreality of this honour may be seen in 1347, when he is again styled bachelor.² For thirty years a judge, he was a man of incredible industry and activity on circuit.

In this way the professional judges of the period helped to swell the ranks of the country gentry. They had to make their way through considerable opposition, because a number of them were self-made men. One sentence given in evidence in the Scrope–Grosvenor controversy³ is worth a volume of social comment: 'I hear it is said that Henry le Scrope [the Chief Justice] is no gentleman, because he is a man of law, and I tell you for certain that his father was knighted at Falkirk and that they are gentlemen and of noble birth.' Like most medieval officials their salaries were nominal and they had to make up their income by acting as private consultants. Like other royal clerks they served the magnates or the monasteries as well as the king.⁴ As Professor E. L. G. Stones has

earlier period. The expenses of Thomas Chaucer and Thomas Stonor as knights of the shire were £47. 12s. No. 258 is a list of 'fencible men' presented by the constables of the half-hundred of Ewelme (about 1480). There were 80 of them, including a constable for each of the seventeen vills—some with 'harness', some armed only with bills, axes, or staves; but only eighteen archers are specified— one to each village.

¹ Bertha Putnam, *William Shareshull* (Cambridge, 1950). The judge lived at Barton Odonis, a liberty of a thousand acres in the parish of Steeplebarton. The home of their ancestors was Barton Abbey in the same parish. Barton Lodge is marked on the sketch maps of the Shareshull estates in Oxon. and Staffs., but not, I think mentioned in the text. On the other hand, Barton Odonis is not on the map.
² Ibid. 32. ³ p. 182.
⁴ I have noted some thirteenth-century examples in *Seignorial Administration*, to which may be added *Ann. Wigorn.* 428, 440, for Mr. William de Poywicke,

shown of Geoffrey le Scrope, they were indispensable and unscrupulous, and hated by the populace.[1] Stapledon was murdered by the London mob in 1326, and the men of law, who held the deeds that proved their servile status, were, as in the French Revolution, singled out for death by the rebels in Kent in 1381.

justice of the forest in 1262, retained *de consilio nostro pro. x. marcis* by Worcester Abbey. See also Sayles, 'Medieval Judges as Legal Consultants', *L.Q.R.* lvi (1940), 247–54, for Ralph de Hengham and Thomas de Cobham, paid an annual fee by Christ Church, Canterbury, and one or two others.

[1] E. L. G. Stones, 'Sir Geoffrey le Scrope (*c.* 1285–1340) Chief Justice of the King's Bench', *E.H.R.* (1954), 1–17.

VI

KNIGHTS IN TOURNAMENT AND AT WAR

THROUGHOUT the fourteenth century the old type of judge persisted, the man trained in tournament and war before he was elevated to the bench. The Chief Justices of both King's Bench and Common Pleas were made knights, but in this age the dignity was by no means a formality, as is typified in the history of the Scrope family, men strenuous in arms, unyielding, litigious, but men of integrity.[1] Geoffrey le Scrope of Masham (d. 1340) had a remarkable career as soldier and diplomat as well as judge. A king's serjeant by 1315, he is said to have been knighted at a tournament at Northampton in September 1323, and in 1324 became Chief Justice of King's Bench. A year or so before he died he was made a banneret with 200 marks a year. His elder brother Henry (d. 1336) was also a Chief Justice (1329) and a very strenuous knight banneret.[2] It was this stalwart Yorkshireman's son Richard who fought at Crécy and Neville's Cross, in the sea-fight near Rye (1350), and with John of Gaunt at Najera, when Don Pedro was restored to the Spanish throne. He led a full life. He was M.P. for Yorkshire in 1364, was summoned to Parliament as a baron in 1371, Treasurer of England from

---

[1] Not all the judges were of this moral stature. The judicial scandal of 1340 was equal in size, and in the severity of the punishments meted out to the delinquents, to that of 1289. In this crisis the king came home in a towering rage from Flanders and visited his wrath upon the administration in general, central and local. All the sheriffs were changed. In 1346 Sir William Thorp, Chief Justice of King's Bench, was charged with accepting bribes and condemned to the Tower of London with loss of his estates.

[2] See E. L. G. Stones, loc. cit.

1371 to 1375, and under Richard II was Steward of the Household. In October 1378 and again in 1381 he was appointed Lord Chancellor. His later years were much occupied by his long-drawn-out controversy with Sir Robert Grosvenor over the right to bear the coat *azure a bend or*, to which his title was amply vindicated, though I find no reason to believe that his opponent's claim was a false one.

In the thirteenth century the great military officers of the Crown, the Constable and the Marshal, who held by Grand Serjeanty, existed to muster, pay, and discipline the armed forces of the king. They acted through a prerogative court that is seen in action in 1322 in the trial of Roger Damory.[1] Their authority was not increased by a commission of 1346 setting up the High Court of Chivalry. Constables in the army had always had a disciplinary power over troops in the field, and the Marshal had had authority over the heralds since the time of William the Marshal. They could hardly prosecute a man for raising his banner in rebellion if they had no authority over what was blazoned on it, so it is possible to believe that the commission of 1346 was simply declaratory, giving special form to an authority that at all times emanated from the fountain of honour.[2] It existed by prescription, though it was not in regular session but grew; like Chancery perhaps, like Admiralty certainly.

The most celebrated case[3] heard and decided in this court in the Middle Ages was that between Sir Richard Scrope of Yorkshire and Sir Robert Grosvenor of Cheshire

[1] T. F. T. Plucknett, 'The Rise of the English State Trial', *Political*, ii. (1937); cited by McKisack, *The Fourteenth Century*, 96, n. 2.

[2] The Court of Star Chamber may be regarded as a parallel instance. See *History and Heraldry*, 120, for differing views on the origins of the Court of Chivalry.

[3] Henry le Scrope is P.R.A. No. 1078. William le Scrope, though dead, is No. 348 in Cotgrave's Ordinary (after 1337), with the purple lion on the bend that the family acquired for services to an Earl of Lincoln. William is said to have been bailiff of the liberty of Richmond, and to have been knighted at the battle of Falkirk in 1298 (*D.N.B.*).

in 1386 over the right to use the arms *azure a bend or*. Before the fourteenth century neither family had achieved more than local importance, and quite possibly they had never met. Neither party figures in the earliest rolls of arms.

The most remarkable feature of this controversy to a modern eye is that no herald was asked to give evidence;[1] neither the royal heralds nor any private herald, nor the rolls made and used by them, are ever mentioned. The only roll that is mentioned was drawn up by a layman and for a layman, Sir John Laton, a north-country knight. It is known that certain heralds existed at this time, but it is a sad reflection upon their standing, at any rate in the Court of Chivalry, that their evidence was not called by either side. Possibly they had found that there was no more in the rolls in their possession than there is in those that survive from that period. The same seems to be true of other heraldic disputes in the Middle Ages.

The upshot of the case, which dragged on for three years, was that Scrope won and was awarded costs, afterwards remitted by him. Grosvenor had been awarded the same arms with a difference, but preferred to change his coat and adopted a garb or wheatsheaf in allusion to the family connection with the Earls of Chester.[2]

In general it may be said that the deponents for Sir Robert Grosvenor were Cheshire men, including a few Welshmen. They were aged 20 to 40 and their evidence was from monumental inscriptions and church windows,[3]

---

[1] The Scrope–Grosvenor Roll was edited in two volumes by 'Harry Nicholas' (Sir Nicholas Harris Nicolas) in 1832. A projected third volume, with notes on some of the Scrope of Bolton depositions and on all the Grosvenor depositions, is still lacking.

[2] The article by C. L. Kingsford in *D.N.B.*, s.v. Grosvenor is useful.

[3] The churches and hall of Over and Nether Poever, churches of Hulme, Moberley, Budworth, Stockport, and St. Werburgh's, Chester, and the Franciscan Convent there. Sir Ralph de Stanleigh deposed, that public report had always said that, in the county of Cheshire and in the neighbourhood, the said arms, etc. In fact they take the matter no further back than the arms on the tomb of Sir Robert Grosvenor's father in the cemetery at Nether Poever (p. 278); also the Abbot of St. Werburgh's, Chester, had seen them on seals of their charters.

KNIGHTS IN TOURNAMENT AND AT WAR 135

with the exception of that from Grosvenor's campaign in Poitou with Lord James Audley, under the Black Prince. It is noteworthy that many of the deponents were relatives of Robert Grosvenor. There seems little doubt that both families had been using the same arms throughout the fourteenth century. The witnesses on both sides had obviously been coached, for there are any number of recurrent stereotyped phrases, running into long periods. It is therefore most refreshing to come upon the testimony of Geoffrey Chaucer, the poet, who describes how he had seen the Scrope arms outside an inn in a London street,[1] and to hear Sir Gervaise Clifton saying that he had been armed for fifty-two years, i.e. since 1334, and that his ancestors frequented tournaments *which were at that time schools of arms and where arms were known*.[2] The depositions do in fact add a few facts to the history of the tournament in the fourteenth century, and the witnesses for Scrope attested in their persons that medieval knights did not always die young. Sir John Sully, a Garter Knight,[3] belonged to a junior branch of the Sullys of Iddesleigh in Devon. In his testimony, which was taken at his home, he said that he was 105 years old and had fought at Halidon Hill and Crécy, and when nearly 90 in 1370 he had had letters of protection for service in Aquitaine. The elder Despenser, Earl of Winchester from 1322, is said to have been executed in 1326 'at the age of 90'. He was in fact 65 (born 1261), but that was a great age for an active knight.

This was not the only *cause célèbre* in the Court of Chivalry at this time. A dispute between Nicholas, Lord

---

[1] Vol. i, 412. [2] Vol. i, 357.
[3] Vol. ii, 240–2: presumably identical with Sir John de Sully, bachelor of the Black Prince's chamber, and a life retainer; from 1352 his fee was increased from £40 to £60 a year 'for the good service he did and the great place which he held on the day of the battle of Poitiers' (*B.P.R.* Cornwall, 45–6, etc.). He was a knight of the shire for Dorset in 1334 and 1352. His arms (Powell's roll No. 502) were *or two bends gules*, as in P.R.A., 864, 874 (Worcs.), 48 Galloway (1300).

Burnell, and Robert, Lord Morley, during the siege of Calais in 1345-8 had repercussions in the case between Thomas, Lord Morley, and John, Lord Lovel of Titchmarsh, over the arms *argent lion rampant sable crowned and armed or*, which the latter claimed in 1386-91 by descent through his grandmother from the Lords Burnell. In this case the judgement was publicly proclaimed by Lancaster Herald. In the Lovell-Morley case of 1295[1] 'Le Roy Vaillant Heraud', aged 60, and 'Le Roy Aquitaigne Heraud', aged 70, both gave 'expert evidence, apparently to the effect that arms can not be given away or alienated'. This is, however, not consonant with the facts. A coat of arms was as much a man's personal property as a roll of other men's arms, and could be devised at will. There exists a licence (*c.* 1317) permitting Edmund D'Eyncourt, who had no male heirs, to alienate his name and arms to whomsoever he willed,[2] and in the Scrope-Grosvenor case it emerged that one of Sir Robert Grosvenor's ancestors gave a parcel of land to William Cotton of Cotton by Chester together with the Grosvenor arms with a difference, possibly as part of a marriage settlement. In spite of these cases the heralds, we are told, began to acquire official standing in the Court of Chivalry only in the fifteenth century.[3]

As a soldier Edward III acted as a magnet for all the chivalrous impulses of his subjects. In the reign of his less warlike father these had often found expression in pilgrimages: e.g. Sir Edmund de Kendale, of the county of Rutland, king's bachelor, went on pilgrimage to Jerusalem 'to accomplish the vow he made when he was in peril in Scotland'.[4] His was a typical county family, other members

---

[1] If I understand Sir Anthony Wagner aright (*Heralds and Heraldry*, 22-3) this was a quite distinct case.
[2] Pat. roll 10 Edward II, part 2, m. 13.
[3] Wagner, *Heralds and Heraldry*, 24.
[4] *Cal. Chancery Warrants*, i. 462 (7 Feb. 1317). In 1323 he was a keeper of the peace in Hants (ibid., 536): cf. *C. Cl. R.* (1318), 338. The chancery clerks of this period do not trouble much to classify men as king's bachelors or king's

becoming knights of the shire, or king's clerks. But under Edward III the energies of these men were concentrated for twenty-one years under the leadership of Henry of Derby, Warwick, Northampton, Suffolk, Reginald Cobham, and Walter Mauny—a record of continuity of command that would be hard to beat in the military history of any age. In these years (1339–60) Edward III had the nation behind him. He was a man of great political sagacity, a fair general, as unscrupulous as his grandfather (cf. the Bardi-Peruzzi débâcle), whose politics were based on similar assumptions to his own, as in his acquisition of baronial estates (Lisle, Pomeray). The *querelae* of 1289–90 are paralleled in 1330.

Many men made fortunes out of the war. Walter Mauny, coming to England as a Hainaulter in 1327, ended up as a baron with land in sixteen counties[1]— he was summoned to Parliament in 1346–7 by individual summons. The Hollands, too, had their share, through a lucky ransom and a secret marriage with the Fair Maid of Kent. Thomas de Holland,[2] a cadet of the Lancashire family, 'won early fame in the tournament, and became what would now be called a millionaire through capturing the Count of Eu at the storming of Caen in 1346'.[3]

To begin with, those who contracted to raise troops for the king made their profits by paying their retainers less than the royal rates, and these retainers became subcontractors and paid in turn less than they received. The ransoms and spoils were divided in different ways, but the contractor never got less than a third. He had to give to the king a share of what he and his men took, and his men

bannerets. This Edmund, or a namesake, was a steward for the Black Prince in Cornwall and the Thames Valley. A relative, Hugh de Kendal, was a wardrobe clerk, Vice-Chancellor, and perhaps clerk of the council.

[1] Article by James Tait in *D.N.B.* xii; and the paper by D. L. Evans in the *Trans. of the Merioneth Historical Society*.

[2] Dugdale, *Bar*. ii. 148–9. He had a manor at Aber in North Wales, about 1338. He died in 1372. His arms are in Cotgrave 159 and Powell 61, *or three chevrons sable*. Cotgrave adds a *lyon passant or* on the middle chevron.

[3] Arthur Bryant, *The Age of Chivalry*, 416.

had to give him a share of what they took.¹ From Freeman's 'joint-stock company' of 1066 to modern protection rackets, everyone must have his cut.

The early fourteenth century, so far as the military service of the country gentry is concerned, saw the completion of the change from status to contract. The royal household, the nucleus of the army, was enlarged in time of war by the retinues of persons not normally attached to it, persons who had contracts, sometimes for life, to serve as occasion required. Some early indentures for service have already been noticed,² and again in 1336 Geoffrey de Say (d. 1359), a banneret of Kent, had a contract, changed in 1349 to a life contract, to serve with four knights, twenty men-at-arms, and twenty archers. He became Admiral of the Fleet from the Thames westwards.³ Lord Henry Percy had in 1331 a life retainder from the Crown for 500 marks a year and the reversion of Warkworth Castle, amount of service unspecified. But his contract with Edward Balliol, King of Scots, in 1333 was to provide a banneret and thirty knights or a hundred men-at-arms, for life, in exchange for 2,000 marks a year in land.⁴ Warenne's retainer of 1,600 marks that comes to light quite incidentally in 1329 is comparable. A few contracts of the time of Edward II are known,⁵ but the flood of agreements under Edward III and Richard II has attracted more attention during the last thirty years.⁶

¹ Donald Hay, 'The Divisions of the Spoils of War in Fourteenth-Century England', *T.R.H.S.*, 5th series, iv (1954), 95 ff.
² *History and Heraldry*, Chap. VI. One of the earliest noted is dated 1300 and comes from Brit. Mus. Add. Ch. 1531, and was made between William Martel and Gilbert de Clare. Cited by Altschul in *The Clare Family*, 1217–1314, 279.
³ *D.N.B.*, s.v. Say.
⁴ *The Percy Chartulary* (Surtees Soc. 1919), 268 ff., 447.
⁵ *C. Cl. R.* (1323), 38 (Thomas de Boulton). The contract made with Ralph Neville was continued by the Crown on Neville's death (*C. Cl. R.* (1327–30), 207).
⁶ The earlier literature may be traced through J. W. Sherborne's article 'Indentured Retinues and English Expeditions to France, 1369–80', *E.H.R.* (1964), 718–46; and texts of numerous contracts are printed by Prof. N. B. Lewis, 'Indentures of Retinue with John of Gaunt, Duke of Lancaster, enrolled

KNIGHTS IN TOURNAMENT AND AT WAR 139

Their bearing on the composition of fourteenth-century armies has been much studied, but they rapidly lose individual interest as their contents become stereotyped.

In 1324 the men-at-arms had been esquires, but in the later years of Edward III men-at-arms included everyone except archers and infantry. By that time the archers were mounted, though earlier they had fought on foot. As the country gentry did not become toxophilites until the late nineteenth century, archery is not a subject that need detain us.

The ratio of bannerets to knights and knights to men-at-arms quite changed in the course of the century, and the personal esquires of the knights can have formed only a small proportion of the total number of men-at-arms. In 1373 the Duke of Lancaster led to France three earls (Stafford, Suffolk, and Warwick), 14 bannerets, 248 knights, 1,766 esquires, and 2,153 archers. Buckingham's expedition of 1380 shows the same proportion, and the last expedition to Brittany in 1375, led by the Duke of Brittany, comprised two earls, two bannerets, 90 knights, 1,895 esquires, and 1,985 archers.

Much has been written about the rich prizes of war in the period 1340–60, but it is also noteworthy that, apart from ransoms, the Black Prince behaved with far greater generosity to those who served him well in war or peace than Edward I had done to persons of similar station.[1] Edward I had lavished corrodies upon retiring members

in Chancery, 1367–99', *Camden Miscellany*, xxii, 4th ser. i, 77–112, and in John of Gaunt's *Register* (1379–81), ed. Armitage-Smith (Camden Soc., 3rd ser.), xx, xxi (1911), and ibid. lvi, lvii (1937), ed. E. C. Lodge and R. Somerville, as Nos. 775–870 in *B.P.R.* i and Nos. 25–35 in *B.P.R.* ii.

[1] Sir John Delves, his 'yeoman' (*valettus*) in 1359, then bachelor as Constable of Denbigh and steward of the lordship, was knighted in 1362 and given 100 marks a year in lands and rents (*B.P.R.* iii, Index). In 1363 he had 6s. 8d. a day more than a banneret—as governor of the Prince's private business. Lord Audley was given 500 marks a year after Poitiers and handed it on to his four esquires, of whom John Delves was one, and each of them was allowed to add part of their lord's arms to his own. Sir John was son of Richard de Delves of Delves Hall near Uttoxeter, Staffs. He became a judge of Common Pleas in 1364 and died in 1369.

of his household at the expense of the Church; the Black Prince paid them off out of his own pocket. When men were being distrained to become knights if they had only £15 a year in land, it must have been a truly rewarding experience to receive (as at least a score did) 100 to 500 marks a year in cash for life. I do not know if the Prince was in a position to have them made corrodars, but, even under the relaxed rules of the later fourteenth century, the kind of knight concerned might not have wished to end his days in a religious house. He was given, at any rate, the option, for he could always buy himself a corrody.

The right to ransom money was not always easy to assess, and so the prisoner was asked for a personal statement. Charles, Count of Dammartin, who was captured at Poitiers, explained how this had come about. He was taken by an esquire of the Prince's household, one John Trailly, to whom he gave his fealty and his bacinet, gauntlets, and sword, Trailly left him in charge of a yeoman and went off to seek further action. A Gascon came and took an escutcheon of the Count's coat armour, i.e. made a note of his coat of arms, or perhaps cut off a piece of his surcoat or his horse's trappings, and left him. Then came another man who led him to the Earl of Salisbury. So whose prisoner was he?[1]

The political significance of the tournament had reached a climax in the early years of Edward II's reign.[2] This phase soon passes, and under royal patronage the tournament becomes even more of a spectacle. Under Edward III, especially during the years between Crécy and Poitiers (1346–56), with the founding of the Order of the Garter, tournaments became, particularly in the form of the

---

[1] *B.P.R.* iv. 339–40.
[2] See *History and Heraldry*, 140; and 'The Tournament in: he Thirteenth Century', *Essays Presented to F. M. Powicke* (1948). Some further references to tournaments will be found in 'Arthurian Influences on Sport and Spectacle', *Arthurian Literature of the Middle Ages*, ed. R. S. Loomis (Clarendon Press, 1959), 553–9, q.v. for continental Round Tables of the thirteenth and fourteenth centuries. The Swan Knight does not appear in this large co-operative work.

Round Table, a function of the monarchy. Windsor, Eltham, and Smithfield were the most favoured places. We hear no more of royal prohibitions, but of licences, expenses, and considerable payments to the Church by way of conscience money.[1] The tournament was in fact one of the more obvious but important ways in which Edward III co-operated with his magnates. If they wanted tournaments, so did the king, for they no longer held the military threat that had necessitated their prohibition. To levy war against the king, a few hundred lances would no longer suffice. Archers, light cavalry, and siege engines would be required and for them the tournament provided no scope. So the tournament, though it could still be lethal,[2] and still open to foul play,[3] was usually no more than a decorative, though still to some a profitable, occasion.

There was a spate of unlicensed tournaments after 1312, hardly interrupted by the defeat at Bannockburn,[4] when once again, as at the turn of the century, men were going abroad to tourney instead of staying at home to fight the Scots. The only exception noted was for the young Earl of Kent, youngest son of Edward I, who was

[1] As at Nefyn in 1284.
[2] *Foed.* II. i. 358 (A.D. 1318). A royal pardon to William Melksop for killing William de Ponton in jousts at Luton, Beds.
[3] In a fight (a judicial combat ?) between Giovanni Visconti and Thomas de la Marche in 1350, 'which was first mounted and then on foot, de la Marche endeavoured to finish off his opponent by means of pricks from the gadlings of his gauntlet' (Maunde Thompson (ed.), *Chronicon Galfridi le Baker de Swynbroke* (1889), 112).
[4] Only four months before Bannockburn there is an order to arrest all persons gone without licence overseas to tourney, and to seize all their lands (*C. Cl. R.* (1313–18), 42 (1 Mar. 1314)). It would be as unprofitable to list all the smaller tournaments recorded in the reign of Edward III as it would be to record all the prohibitions issued by his father. Both run into scores. In Sept. 1313 it was particularly the insurgent earls at Brackley in Northampton who caused alarm (*C. Cl. R.* (1313–18), 68–9, 70–1) and it is from about this time that men-at-arms or *armigeri* (esquires) are mentioned in the writs among the participants. In 1317–18 there are half a dozen detailed general prohibitions to all counties (ibid. 42, 86, 388, 445, 536, 570). There can be little doubt that these prohibitions of Edward II were ineffective.

given permission to tourney at Northampton on the Sunday after Michaelmas 1323, notwithstanding a prohibition of 6 August.[1] It was probably on this occasion, and not at an unlicensed meeting, that the future judge, Geoffrey le Scrope, was knighted.[2]

The prohibitions continued to the end of the reign,[3] and thus reveal, incidentally, the prevalence of unlicensed meetings, which presumably had the added attraction of illicit sport, as later with prize-fighting and cock-fights. With the added power of Queen Isabella and her paramour Roger Mortimer, the old Marcher tradition was revived and Round Tables were held at Bedford (1328) and at Hereford for the marriage of Mortimer's daughter, when the Queen Mother was present.[4]

[1] *C. Cl. R.* (1323–7), 136 (the licence of 28 Aug. 1323 and the prohibition of 6 Aug.).

[2] This is an important date in the history of the Scrope family. The tournament at Northampton, and there were not many there, is placed firmly in the reign of Edward II by the evidence of Sir William Alton and Sir John Rither (*Scrope–Grosvenor Controversy*, i. 142–3; ii. 350, 352). Sir John was born only about 1320, and the tournament took place in 1323. It was prohibited, but this was common form, and the tournament was held none the less. Prof. E. L. G. Stones in *E.H.R.* (1954), 2–3, n. 10, gives details from Stowe MS. 553, fols. 128, 130, a wardrobe book of this year. Scrope took £26. 13*s*. 4*d*. in aid of his expenses. In any case Scrope was knighted in Sept. 1323, when he became a puisne judge of Common Pleas. Sir Thomas Roos of Kendale, aged over 80 in 1386, said in his evidence in the Scrope–Grosvenor case (vol. i, p. 132) that he had seen Sir Geoffrey Scrope 'armed in the same arms' (*azure a bend or*), *e ceo en penoun*, at Stannow Park (Feb. 1328), i.e. before he was made a banneret. After describing Sir William Scrope as the most able tourneyour of his time, the deponent continued that he saw Sir Geoffrey Scrope in tournaments at Guildford and Newmarket; and at Dunstable in the time of Edward III, who was present. This would be the occasion of the second Dunstable roll of arms, made in 1334 when the magnates met the king there and staged the tournament in his honour. Foss, in his *Judges of England*, makes the unfortunate remark, followed by Sir Harris Nicholas, that Scrope displayed his *banner and pennon* at the affair of Stannow Park (vol. i, p. 99).

[3] *C. Cl. R.* (23 July 1323), 129. Against any earl, baron, etc., at Southwell Notts., or elsewhere within the realm without special licence; and again in general form, and including perhaps for the first time men-at-arms or esquires, in 1326 (12 Dec., ibid. 658).

[4] Mary Griffin, 'Cadwallader, Arthur, and Brutus in the Wigmore MS.', *Speculum*, xvi (1941), 109–20, citing Knighton, i. 449; and see Geoffrey le Baker, 42.

There was, however, an edict at Westminster early in 1327 that no tournaments, bourds, jousts, and so forth should be held without special licence,[1] and breakers of this could, after 1328, be brought under the Statute of Northampton.

The execution of the Earl of Kent in March and of Roger Mortimer on 29 November 1330 had no more effect upon the fashionable pastime than the murder of Gaveston had had in 1312. But from 1331 they were held with the sanction of the Crown.[2] Queen Isabella of Hainault enjoyed them too, but had the misfortune to fall from a grandstand at Cheapside with many of her ladies. Some, perhaps many, of the ladies were hurt, but the Queen apparently escaped injury.[3]

Few tournaments have been recorded between 1331 and 1342, except for those at Langley, Reading, and Dunstable in 1341,[4] and the better-known solemnity which was the occasion of the second Dunstable roll of arms in 1334. If there had been any of importance they would hardly have escaped Murimuth or Geoffrey le Baker.

In 1342, after Christmas at Melrose, Edward III intended to fight the Scots, but they hid behind the Forth and he could do no more than lay waste the Lowlands and take much booty. Some knights on both sides agreed on a tournament, with the king's licence, and a few on each side were killed, so they made a truce till Lent.[5] This year, however, does provide a tournament of great interest in that it reveals the true nature of the matter. It was only in international tournaments that people really wanted to

---

[1] *C. Cl. R.* (1327–30), 47, 105, 107, 231, 376, 382, 389, 402, 403, 407, 544, 547; (1330–3), 52, 147, 286, 301, 303, 397, all of which refer to the necessity of a licence.

[2] Mur. 63 (Dartford, late Apr. 1331), also in le Baker, 49, and *Ann. Paulin.*, 354–5.

[3] Rob de Avesbury, 286 (about Michaelmas); Bridlington Annals, 112.

[4] Le Baker, 75.

[5] Mur. 123.

kill each other. At other times, if death supervened, it was usually by accident. The contestants, however, did covet each other's horses, the prize of the victor, and it was at all times an outrage to injure a horse rather than its rider. These points are well illustrated by the Dunstable tournament held in 1342 on Monday before the beginning of Lent.[1] It was slightly larger than the first or second Dunstable tournaments, which show 235 and 135 combatants respectively, since we are told that 250 knights took part. All the young earls were there—Derby, Warwick, Northampton, Pembroke, and Suffolk—but age and infirmity excused Gloucester, Arundel, Devon, Warenne, and Huntingdon. The king took part as a simple knight, i.e. as a knight bachelor. There were no aliens, and apparently no casualties. The coming of night put a stop to the fighting, so that *barely ten horses were lost or won*. Again, about 24 June 1343, there was jousting for three whole days at Smithfield by London at the proclamation of Sir Robert de Morley, *without harm or injury to anyone*. Here the 'Pope' and twelve 'cardinals' all dressed alike upheld the 'interior' party for three courses against all comers, presumably in defence of some temporary wooden structure. The Prince of Wales, and many earls, barons, knights, and esquires took part. The Earl of Warwick carried off the prize.[2]

Edward III's great tournament at Windsor on 19 January 1343/4 was publicized on the Continent as well as in England. For a similar affair in 1359 heralds were sent to France, Germany, Brabant, Flanders, and Scotland. The *tirocinium* on St. George's Day (19 January) did much to establish the cult of that saint in England. If I understand his career aright, St. George was a

---

[1] Mur. 123-4, and App. 223. A fortnight after Easter there were jousts at Northampton, when many nobles were seriously injured and John de Beaumont killed. The Queen's brother, the Count of Hainault, arrived in England about Whitsuntide, and jousts were held at Eltham in Kent.

[2] Mur. 146, and App. 230-1. After this many jousts were held at Canterbury, Hereford, and elsewhere, but the king found recreation in hunting.

war profiteer in Cappadocia, and set temporal before spiritual riches in his handling of army contracts. But he made a better go of it than his followers in the mid fourteenth century, some of whom acquired riches, but like Pulteney and his fellows were discovered and impeached; one—de la Pole—was ennobled, but none attained the honours of sanctity. This *tirocinium* then was widely advertised, as messengers were paid only a few pence a day, and their expenses were £32.[1] The tournament at Nefyn in 1284 had also been an international affair. In 1359 the occasion was the marriage of John of Gaunt to Blanche of Lancaster, when the king, his four sons, and nineteen nobles, disguised as the major and aldermen, tilted in London against all comers.[2]

For a score of years (1340–60) tournaments proliferated and heralds abounded. Ladies were usually present, and, to revert to the great occasion of 1343/4, all the ladies of the south of England and the wives of the citizens of London were invited. A banquet to which no men were invited except two knights from France was arranged in the great hall of Windsor. Queen Philippa, Isabella, the Queen Mother, nine countesses, and the wives of barons, knights, and burgesses were there, the seating being arranged by the king himself. The Prince of Wales, the Earl of Cornwall, the earls, barons, knights and the rest had their dinner in a marquee in the courtyard. This is a curious feature for which no reason is given, but it was perhaps an anticipation of the habit of a later age whereby the men were left to their port and cigars whilst the ladies

[1] Cited by Jusserand, *Wayfaring Life*, 229, from the *Issues of the Exchequer* (1837), 169. These may have been 'the jousts which the Earl of la Marche caused to be proclaimed after the feast of Windsor in 32 Edward III' (*B.P.R.* iv, 323). The Black Prince returned from Gascony and spent £2 on ostrich feathers for the jousts at Smithfield this year (ibid. 284) and John, Duke of Brittany, received a royal warrant for his expenses at the tournament there (*Foed.* III. i. 421). This is one of the few occasions in which the king actually took part, as in 1358 at Smithfield and Cheapside, with the kings of France and Scotland (ibid. 129).

[2] John of Reading, 152, 156.

sat apart in the withdrawing-room. There was dancing and song for three days, during which the king personally with nineteen knights jousted against all comers. On the first day Sir Miles de Stapelton was adjudged the winner (*gratias reportavit*), on the second Philip Despenser, and on the third John Blount. On the fourth day the king held a great feast at which he inaugurated his Round Table and received the oaths of certain earls, barons, and knights whom he wished to be of the Order.[1] The numbers here and elsewhere when the Round Table is mentioned preclude the idea of anything but a series of trestle tables, quite apart from the fact that 'to hold a Round Table' means not merely to waive the rules of precedence, but more generally to have a feast and jousts and indulge in other sports and festivities, in which according to some modern writers there was a certain amount of promiscuity. Another Round Table was arranged for Whitsuntide and a special building was ordered to be erected, but work was stopped by the necessity of diverting all available moneys to the war in France.

This Round Table did not see the inauguration of the Order of the Garter, 'the knights of which wore their insignia for the first time at a tournament at Eltham in January 1348, when nine of the original founders jousted before the king, among them the Prince of Wales, Henry of Lancaster, the Constable of Northampton, and the young Earl of Salisbury'.[2] The Order is said to have been formally constituted during the course of the nineteen tournaments held that winter and spring at Bury St. Edmunds and Eltham, at Canterbury, Lichfield, and

[1] Mur. 155–6. App., 231, explains '... in the same manner as King Arthur, to wit to the number of 300 knights', including of course Derby, Salisbury, Warwick, Arundel, Pembroke, and Suffolk. But Salisbury (William de Montague) had been wounded in the jousts and died a week later.

[2] Sir Arthur Bryant, *The Age of Chivalry*, 324. Mantles and *Honi soit qui mal y pense* garters were issued for the king and twelve companions. The Chapel of St. Edward was redecorated as the Chapel of St. Edward and St. George, Windsor.

Lincoln, and at Windsor for the churching of the Queen after the birth of her youngest son.[1] But the office of Garter Principal King of Arms was first created in 1415 by Henry V, just before he sailed for France. Thus the institution of the Order was complete by 1348, but how far the stories connected with it are to be believed, such as the one of the Countess of Salisbury's garter and the unhappy tale of the poor knights of Windsor, is a matter, like the rise of freemasonry, best left to the historians of the mystery.

A comparison of the events of 1306 and 1344 is all in Edward III's favour. He had the advantage of youth, for Edward I was an old man at the Feast of the Swans, a knight over forty years in arms, as a Scrope or Grosvenor witness might have said. The intention of each was probably the same, to encourage a spirit of martial endeavour among the nobles and their followers in close association with the king. In 1344 Edward III, according to Murimuth, writing contemporaneously in London, won three of the six prizes in the jousts at Windsor. He made a formal announcement in the royal chapel at Windsor, in the presence of the Steward (Derby), the Marshal (Salisbury), the Black Prince, and the Queen, and swore to renew the Round Table of Arthur with 300 knights.

This is the culmination of a series of acts that completely reversed royal policy towards jousting and the tourney. There were no half-measures. In 1344 the king had gone so far as to grant a perpetual licence to the citizens of Lincoln for *hastiludia sive justas* each year in war and peace.[2] This policy had been foreshadowed from time to time by Edward I, and the strong flow of prohibitions under Edward II merely showed that the king was not strong enough to enforce a policy in which he had little interest.

[1] Margaret Galway, 'Joan of Kent and the Order of the Garter', *Birmingham University Historical Journal*, vol. i. The tournament at Lincoln was held by Lancaster (Geoffrey le Baker, 98).   [2] *Foed*. III. i. 5.

148 KNIGHTS IN TOURNAMENT AND AT WAR

There were at this time many local tournaments that are only recorded for some unusual feature, such as the arbitrary behaviour of Sir John Daniel, one of the Black Prince's bachelors, who in 1352 proclaimed a tournament at Warrington for which he stole the torches of the parson Roger of Chester, rector of Grappenhall.[1] Next year one was staged at Smithfield for the entertainment of the Breton prisoners, who were afterwards sent home.[2] On all such occasions when the Black Prince, who had his own king of arms,[3] was present, he was lavish in his gifts to minstrels, heralds, the knights of his companionship, and in alms to the four orders of friars as well as to anchorites, especially in the decade 1350–60.[4]

The rules for these encounters, the first heard of since the Statute of Arms in the thirteenth century, were elaborated and reissued in the name of Thomas of Woodstock, one of the younger sons of Edward III, Constable of England 1376–97.[5] Froissart (*sub anno* 1390) gives the rules about touching the shield of an opponent in challenge. There was, indeed, a royal tournament that year at Woodstock, as recorded by Dugdale in his *Baronage*.[6] It is noteworthy that in all the actual contests described no

[1] *B.P.R.* iii. 59. Sir John was retained for one year from 1 Aug. 1359 for 70 marks, with three squires, for good service at Poitiers. Sir Thomas Daniel, also the Prince's bachelor, had 40 marks a year for taking prisoner the Chamberlain of Tankerville and replanting the Prince's banner at the battle of Crécy (ibid. i. 45, 48).

[2] Robert of Avesbury, 419.

[3] As Duke of Acquitaine, the Black Prince had his own king of arms. In 1375 Nicholas Duchayn acted in this capacity, and must have been well paid as he could afford to lend £20 sterling to John of Gaunt (John of Gaunt's *Register*, ii, No. 1609).

[4] *B.P.R.* iv. 67, 73, 124, 324, 428. And to the following heralds named in the Index: Mosseron (and variants); Faucon; Hameray; John of Lancaster; William de Stafford, herald of arms of Alvan; and Godkyn, herald of Gollerland.

[5] The original French version is printed in the *Black Book of the Admiralty*, ed. Sir Travers Twiss (R.S. 1872) i. 328, and the fifteenth-century version is in *Archaeologia*, lvii, pt. I, App. B, p. 61. The rules made by John, Lord Tiptoft, Earl of Worcester and Constable of England, 29 May, 6 Edw. IV, are printed by F. H. Cripps-Day, *The History of the Tournament* (1918), App. iv, p. xxvii.

[6] *Baronage*, i. 58.

one is named as judge who awards the prizes, except Edward III when present, though in Chaucer's imaginary (about 1380?) mêlée of 100 v. 100 there is a referee Theseus, who shrewdly decides that honour has been done and that the result is a draw.

But it was not long after this that the fully mailed knight became an anachronism in England, though he had yet to fight at Agincourt, and survived another century. Even in 1400 the armour of Guy, Earl of Warwick, who had died in 1315, was piously bequeathed for the third time.[1]

[1] Cripps-Day, op. cit. 49-50.

APPENDIX I

The Caerlaverock and Galloway Rolls

MUSTER rolls sound like a promising source of information for heralds about to prepare occasional rolls, but when the test is made it is found that their value is strictly limited. No rolls, of course, except those made by heralds, give any heraldic information. Secondly, though a mid-thirteenth-century roll may have included all the cavalry, when the indenture or contract system took root the records relating to a muster became much more complicated; but a muster roll remains a record of feudal services proffered and accepted in return for land held by knight service or in serjeanty, and this is all that the Carlisle muster roll of June 1300 has to offer. It may be that the 'chronicles of great musters' cited in the first lines of the Caerlaverock poem are really a number of documents, not merely a single muster roll. For the Constable, who was responsible, and the Marshal, who kept the records in the Marshalsey, had not only to value the horses and make horse-inventories, but also to collect indentures or contracts of service between the king and his captains, if they had chosen to serve *ad vadia*. The roll of the host for the siege of Caerlaverock, though mustered at Carlisle on 25 June 1300 before Humphrey de Bohun, Earl of Hereford and Essex, Constable of England, also contains notices of the appearances of military tenants in person or by deputies from 15 June to 2 July.[1] This roll shows 191 tenants proffering 281 knight's fees and twenty sergeants mustering 445 horsemen, mostly light cavalry or sergeants *cum equo discoperto*, and Sir James Ramsay, noticing the discrepancy between these numbers and the references to 3,000 men-at-arms in the Caerlaverock poem,[2] suggested that more may have been raised by contract. The matter is unfortunately not so simple as that, for only twenty-nine names from the muster roll are found in the poem's hundred or so bannerets. Fuller information would come from the horse inventories as at Falkirk, together with the file of indentures and lists of those

[1] F. Palgrave, *Documents relating to Scotland* (1832), 209–31.
[2] *Dawn of the Constitution*, 472.

who served in person, had made fine, had sent deputies, or were already serving under contract or *ad vadia* in the March, or for wages in the royal household.

So if our herald-ministral saw only the existing muster roll, he would still have had the formidable task of finding out who the other seventy bannerets were. It seems only common sense to suppose that captains of troops knew whom they were leading and had lists of them, just as the wardrobe kept lists of cavalry officers who had to be paid. By this time the muster rolls only records about one-third of the army, the feudal third, so, in spite of the first line of the poem of Caerlaverock, the herald is not dependent upon the muster roll of Carlisle for his list of bannerets. Little is heard of the 600 or so bachelors, each with a number of esquires and sergeants, who together made up the 3,000 men-at-arms mentioned. So for every man mentioned we must imagine thirty in support, plus the innumerable infantry and archers; and the siege engines that made victory possible.

Galloway Roll (1300)

After the capture of Caerlaverock Castle on 15 July 1300, while the king was staying at Twynholm (1–5 August) just west of Kirkcudbright, where he had been from 19 to 27 July, there was a skirmish in which Robert Keith, the Marshal of Scotland, was captured. Next day the whole English army reached the Cree and found the Scots facing them across the tidal estuary. When the tide went out, the English infantry crossed over, 'presumably between Creetown and Newton Stewart'. Edward had not intended to follow, but owing to a misunderstanding the Earl of Hereford's brigade went over, so the king and his sons followed. They had unfortunately no Welsh infantry, which was accustomed to this kind of terrain, to engage the enemy in pursuit.[1] The skirmish at Cree (8 August) has provided us with an occasional roll of some interest. It has not been mentioned by historians, nor does it add to our knowledge of this confused and unusual type of action in which cavalry were sent into aid a misconceived infantry attack, except in so far as it records the name of those engaged. The roll does not include Warenne, who followed the king, nor Hereford, who was sent to recall the foot. It is a mixed roll running bannerets

---

[1] I follow closely Prof. G. W. S. Barrow's account (based largely on Rishanger, *Chron.* 442) in his *King Robert Bruce* (1965), 157–60.

and bachelors together. The whole army of Caerlaverock is not here. Of the vanguard (Lincoln) only Richard de Huddleston le Fils (C. 11, G. 240), is present. The second brigade (Warenne) is not here at all, though Warenne himself is said to have followed the king across the ford (of the Nith). The third or king's brigade at Caerlaverock here lacks Ellis d'Aubigny (No. 35), Maurice de Craon (No. 39), and Simon de Montague (No. 65). The fourth brigade at Caerlaverock (the Prince's) here lacks Richard, Earl of Arundel (No. 80), Alan la Zouche (No. 81), Robert de Willoughby (No. 92), John of Wigton (No. 99), and Richard of Kirkbride (No. 100).

Apart from the Lancaster brothers (Nos. 201, 211), Earl Patrick (Lennoz) and his son (Nos. 35, 38), Gloucester (Ralph Morthermer, No. 218), and John of Brittany (No. 28), who was created Earl of Richmond in 1306, the earls are not on this roll.

Only half the army of Caerlaverock was present. The number of bachelors is less than might have been expected—74 bannerets and only 185 bachelors. How many 'men-at-arms' or 'esquires' were present is not known, but the herald-ministrel suggests 3,000 at Caerlaverock, not the numbers of the infantry.[1]

Stirling Roll (1304)

The names on the Stirling Roll appear to form a genuine list of persons present at the siege of Stirling Castle in 1304 (22 April–20(?) July).[2] But the heading of the sixteenth-century transcript is

[1] Coll. of Arms MS. 14 ff. 75, 168 The Galloway Roll exists only in this copy made by Sir Thomas Wriothesley, Garter (d. 1534). It contains 260 names divided under two headings, 'La Bataille le bon Roy Edouard en Galway en Essoce l'an de son règne xxviii' (Nos. 1–157) and 'La Bataile le Filz le Roy' (Nos. 158–260).

Details of the retinues, valuable to the antiquary and genealogist, will be found in P.R.O. E 101/8/26, and some are printed in *Liber Quotidianus Garderobae Regis* (Soc. of Antiquaries, 1780). A modern edition of this most confusing document is much needed. The accounts were actually made up in 1306 (98, 99) from earlier material (210). The heaviest payments were to John de St. John, £272 in wages (p. 200), £244 *in restauro equorum* (p. 176), and £413. 12s. as Captain and Warden of the Marches for '*secret expenses*' by order of King and Council at Westminster, 1 February 1300'.

[2] *C.E.M.R.A.*, 36. We are dependent, as for the Galloway Roll, on Coll. of Arms MS. 14 ff. 269–72 (made before 1534). The confusion created by the heading of the roll caused Camden in 1614 to relate it to the battle of Stirling Bridge, 1297 (ibid. xxi).

misleading. It may be an addition of that date (though this seems unlikely) or earlier, but in any case made by one who was unable in his mind to distinguish between the battle of Stirling Bridge on 11 September 1297 and the siege of the castle in 1304. The former was an English defeat, unlikely to be celebrated in an English roll, but the siege resulted in the capture of the castle.

The heading says that the English crossed the river after eating, and, finding the enemy drawn up on the banks, put them to flight. The roll itself is incomplete and gives merely the names of ninety-three persons in the vanguard under the Earl of Hereford, and nine in the king's brigade on 30 May 1304. The confusion lies in placing the Scots, who were in the castle under Sir William Oliphant, on the banks of the river outside the town, and in making them flee. Everything else seems quite appropriate to 1304.

APPENDIX II

A Fourteenth-Century Knight-Errant: Sir Giles de Argentine

SIR GILES DE ARGENTINE, a cadet of the house of Argentine,[1] was one of the most zealous jousters of the age. He was only an esquire at Falkirk in 1298,[2] but by 1302 had already been imprisoned for tourneying contrary to a royal prohibition. On being freed to fight the Scots, he deserted and went jousting at Byfleet with six other barons, for which he was again ordered to be imprisoned.[3] As 'King of the Greensward' he held the field against all comers at Stepney in 1308.[4] The family arms (Collins's Roll No. 175) were 'three covered cups Argent' and the younger Giles bore this, with the field semée with cross-crosslets as his difference, at the first Dunstable tournament (No. 7). He was a Cambridgeshire knight: his grandfather had been baron of Bottisham, Cambridgeshire (d. 1283/4), but had forfeited his barony in 1265 (Dugdale, *Bar. s.v.*). He had been Steward of the Household in 1260, and as a rebel had served on the baronial councils of twenty-four, twelve, and nine.

In Sir Thomas Grey of Heton's *Scalacronica* the younger Giles is described as the best knight in Christendom. He served abroad with Henry of Luxemburg, then went to Scotland and

[1] Argentine is in Poitou. The descent seems to be thus:

Giles, d. 1283/4
|
Reynold, baron by writ 1283, d. 1307/8
(*Cal. I.P.M. V*, No. 40)
|
John, aged 30+ in 1308. (*P.R.A.* 95)
|
John (I Dunst. 128, with Earl of Lancaster)

Giles (P.R.A. 593 Camb.). (Gough, *Scotland in 1298*, p. 109).

[2] H. Gough, loc. cit.
[3] *C. Cl. R.* (1302–7), 66.
[4] *Ann. Lond.* i. 157; *Ann. Paulin.* i. 267 (28 May 1308).

SIR GILES DE ARGENTINE

was leader of the king's personal bodyguard at the battle of Bannockburn. After seeing the king safely off the field he returned to the fight, declaring that his honour would not allow him to flee, and plunged suicidally into the forest of Scottish spears.[1]

The importance of Giles in the estimation of the king is shown when in 1313 Giles had been captured at Rhodes by the *malveisins* of that island, and imprisoned at Salonica. The king wrote to the Master of the Hospital, the *podestà* of Genoa, Andronicus, Emperor of Constantinople, and his son Michael, to the Marquess of Montferrat, Frederick, King of Sicily, the Count of Lavagna, as well as to some cardinals and other notables.[2]

[1] Barrow, *Bruce*, 327, citing the *Scalacronica* (ed. for the Maitland Club, 1836) and Barbour's *Bruce*, 235.
[2] *C. Cl. R.* (7 Aug. 1313), 71, 76 (and in *Foedera*).

LIST OF WORKS CITED

ALTSCHUL, MICHAEL. *A Baronial Family in Medieval England: The Clares, 1217–1314* (Oxford University Press, 1965).
Annales monasterii de Bermundeseia, in *Annales monastica*, vol. iii (R.S.).
Annales prioratus de Dunstaplia, in *Annales monastica*, vol. iii (R.S.).
Annales Londonienses, in *Chronicles of the Reigns of Edward I and II* (R.S.).
Annales monasterii de Oseneia, in *Annales monastica*, vol. iv (R.S.).
Annales Paulini in *Chronicles of the Reigns of Edward I and II*, vol. i. 253–370.
Annales monasterii de Theokesberia, in *Annales monastica*, vol. i (R.S.).
AULT, WARREN, D., *Private Jurisdiction in England* (1926).
AVESBURY, ROBERT OF, *De Gestis mirabilibus regis Edwardi tertii*, ed. E. M. Thompson (R.S. 1889).
BAKER, GEOFFREY LE, *Chronicon Galfridi le Baker de Swynbroke*, ed. E. M. Thompson (1889).
BALDWIN, JAMES, *The King's Council* (1912).
BARROW, G. W. S., *King Robert Bruce* (1965).
BELLAMY, J. G., 'The Coterel Gang: An Anatomy of a Band of Fourteenth-century Criminals', *E.H.R.* (1964), 698–717.
Black Book of the Admiralty, ed. Sir Travers Twiss (R.S. 1872).
Black Prince's Register, four volumes (P.R.O., 1930–3).
BLISS, *Calendar Papal Letters*, Vol. i.
'Boroughbridge Roll', ed. J. Greenstreet, *The Genealogist*, N.S. i (1884) and ii (1885). See vol. xxi for an article on the battle of Boroughbridge by the Hon. Vicary Gibbs.
Bridlington, a canon of, *Gesta Edwardi de Carnarvon*, ed. W. Stubbs, in *Chronicles of the Reigns of Edward I and II* (R.S. 1882–3).
BRYANT, SIR ARTHUR, *The Age of Chivalry* (1963).
BURNE, A. H., *The Creçy War* (London, 1955).
Calendar of Chancery Warrants.
Calendar of Close Rolls.

LIST OF WORKS CITED

Calendar of Fine Rolls.
Calendar of Inquisitions Post Mortem.
Cal. Miscellaneous Inquisitions.
Calendar of Patent Rolls.
CAM, HELEN, 'The Legislators of Medieval England' (Ralegh Lecture, 1945), *Proc. Brit. Acad.* xxxi. 132–58.
—— *Liberties and Communities in Medieval England* (Cambridge, 1944).
CAMPBELL, MILDRED, *The English Yeomen* (Merlin Press, 1960).
CHAUCER, GEOFFREY, *The Canterbury Tales: the Prologue.*
CLARK, G. T., 'Poll Tax Returns for the West Riding of Yorkshire, 1379', *Y.A.J.* vii (1882).
CLARKE, M. V., *Representation and Consent* (1936).
—— *Fourteenth-Century Studies* (1937).
COOKE, A. H., *The Early History of Mapledurham* (Oxfordshire Rec. Soc. iii, 1925).
CRIPPS-DAY, F. H., *The History of the Tournament* (1918).
DELBROUILLE, MAURICE, *Le Tournoi de Chauvençy*, Bibl. de la Faculté de Philosophie et Lettres de l'Université de Liège. Fasc. xlix (1932).
DENHOLM-YOUNG, N., *Cartulary of the Mediaeval Archives of Christ Church, Oxford* (Oxford Hist. Soc., 1931).
—— and H. Kantorowicz, 'De Ornatu Mulierum', in *Bibliofilia* (1933).
—— *Seignorial Administration in England* (Oxford, 1937).
—— 'Caversins and Merchants of Cahors', in *Medievalia et Humanistica* (1946).
—— *Richard of Cornwall* (Blackwell, 1947).
—— 'The Tournament in the Thirteenth Century', in *Essays Presented to Frederick Maurice Powicke* (Oxford, 1948).
—— 'The *Liber Epistolaris*' of Richard de Bury (Roxburghe Club, 1950).
—— 'The Authorship of the Vita Edwardi Secundi', *E.H.R.* (1956).
—— *History and Heraldry, 1254–1310* (Oxford, 1965).
Dictionary of Welsh Biography (English edn., 1959).
Dictionary of National Biography.
DUGDALE, SIR WILLIAM, *The Baronage of England*, 2 vols., 1675–6.
EDWARDS, J. G. [now Sir Goronwy], 'The Personnel of the

Commons in the Reign of Edward II', *Essays Presented to Thomas Frederick Tout* (Manchester, 1925), 197–215.

EDWARDS, J. G., *Calendar of Ancient Correspondence Relating to Wales* (Cardiff, 1935).

—— 'The Treason of Thomas Turberville', in *Essays in Medieval History presented to Frederick Maurice Powicke* (Oxford, 1948).

—— 'Castle-Building in Wales', in *Proc. Brit. Acad.* for 1946 (publ. 1951).

—— *The Commons in Medieval English Parliaments* (London, 1958).

The English Government at Work, 1327–1336, vols. i and ii, ed. J. F. Willard and W. A. Morris (Cambridge, Mass., 1940); vol. iii, ed. Willard, Morris, and W. H. Dunham (1950).

Essex, Medieval (Essex County Council Publications, 2nd edn. 1964).

EVANS, D. L. [now Sir David], 'Some Notes on the History of the Principality [of Wales] in the time of the Black Prince', *Trans. Hon. Soc. of Cymmrodorion* (1925–6), 25–100.

—— *Flintshire Ministers' Accounts, 1328–53* (1929).

—— 'The Later Middle Ages (1282–1536)', *The History of Carmarthenshire*, ed. J. E. Lloyd (Cardiff, 1935), 201–67.

—— 'Walter de Mauny, Sheriff of Merioneth, 1332–72', *Journal of the Merioneth Hist. and Rec. Soc.* iv, pt. iii, 194–203.

EVANS, JOAN, *Medieval English Art* (vol. 5 in the *Oxford History of English Art*) (1949).

FARRER, W., *Early Yorkshire Charters*, vols. i–iii; vols. iv ff. in progress, ed. C. T. (now Sir Charles) Clay.

Fees, The Book of, 1198–1293 (P.R.O. calendars), ed. Sir H. Maxwell-Lyte (superseding the *Testa de Nevill*, ed. 1807 Rec. Comm.), 3 vols. (1920–31).

FLETCHER, BANNISTER, *A History of Architecture on the Comparative Method*, 17th edn. revised (1965) by R. A. Cordingley.

Foedera, ed. Thomas Rymer and others (Record Commission, 1816 ff.).

Flores Historiarum (R.S.).

FOWLER, G. H., *Rolls from the Office of the Sheriff of Beds. and Bucks.* (Beds. Rec. Soc. 4°, 1929).

FROISSART, *Chroniques*. See McKisack, *The Fourteenth Century*, p. 548 for edd.

GALE, R. C., *Powell's Roll*, ed. for the Society of Genealogists (1963).

Galloway Roll of Arms (A.D. 1300) = College of Arms MS. 14 ff. 168–75.

GALWAY, MARGARET, 'Joan of Kent and the Order of the Garter', *Birmingham University Hist. Journal*, i.

GAUNT, JOHN OF, *Register*, ed. Armitage-Smith, Camden Soc., 3rd ser., xx, xxi (1911); and E. C. Lodge and R. Somerville, ibid. lvi, lvii (1937).

G.E.C. = *The Complete Peerage*, by G. E. Cokayne, new edn. by V. Gibbs and others (1910 ff).

GIBSON, S. T., 'The Escheatries, 1323–41', *E.H.R.* (1921).

GRAVESEND, *The Register of Richard Gravesend, Bishop of Lincoln* (1258–79), ed. F. N. Davis and others (Cant. and York Soc., 1925).

—— *The Register of Stephen Gravesend, Bishop of London* (1313–38), ibid. (1911), ed. R. E. Fowler.

GREENSTREET, J. *Powell's Roll (c. A.D. 1350)*, in Jewitt's *Reliquary* (N.S.), iii (1889) and iv (1890). See also Gale.

GRIFFIN, MARY, 'Cadwallader, Arthur, and Brutus in the Wigmore MS.', *Speculum*, xvi (1941), 109–20.

HAY, DONALD, 'The Division of the Spoils of War in Fourteenth-Century England', *T.R.H.S.*, 5th ser., iv (1954), 95 ff.

HEMINGBURGH, WALTER DE, *Chronicle* (1048–1346), ed. H. C. Hamilton (Eng. Hist. Soc., 1849) and H. Rothwell (Camden Soc. 1957).

HOBHOUSE, BISHOP, *Calendar of the Register of John de Droxford, bishop of Bath and Wells, 1309–1329* (Somerset Record Soc., 1887).

HUNNISETT, R. F., *The Medieval Coroner* (C.U.P., 1961).

JENKINSON, H., and MILLS, MABEL M., 'Rolls from a Sheriff's Office in the Fourteenth Century', *E.H.R.* (1928), 21–33.

JOLLIFFE, J. E. A., 'The Castles as Local Receipts under King John', in *Essays presented to Frederick Maurice Powicke* (Oxford, 1948).

JUSSERAND, J. J., *English Wayfaring Life in the Middle Ages*, 3rd edn. (1925).

KAYE, J. M., *Placita Corone* or *la Corone Pledae devant Justices* (Selden Soc., Suppl. Ser., vol. iv, 1967).

KENDALL, PAUL MURRAY, *The Yorkist Age* (London, 1962).

KER, N., *Medieval Libraries of Great Britain* (R. Hist. Soc., 2nd edn., 1964).

KING, GREGORY, *Natural and Political Observations upon the State and Condition of England, 1696* (publ. in 1801 with additions by George Chalmers).
KINGSFORD, C. L. (ed.), *The Stonor Papers* (Camden Soc., 4th ser., 1919–20).
KNOWLES, M. David, *The Religious Orders in England*, vol. ii (Cambridge, 1955).
Lanercost Chronicle [to 1346], ed. J. Stevenson (Edinburgh, 1839).
LAPSLEY, GAILLARD, 'Buzones', *E.H.R.* (1947), 177–193, 545–67.
—— 'The Commons and the Statute of York', *E.H.R.* xxviii (1913), 118–24.
LEADMAN, D. H., 'The Battle of Boroughbridge', *Y.A.J.* vii (1882).
LEWIS, N. B., 'Indentures of Retinue with John of Gaunt, Duke of Lancaster, enrolled in Chancery, 1367–99', *Camden Miscellany*, 4th ser., i. 77–112.
Liber Quotidianus Garderobe Regis (Soc. of Antiquaries, 1780).
LODGE, E. C., and THORNTON, G. A., *English Constitutional Documents, 1307–1485* (1935).
LONDON, H. STANFORD, 'Early Treatises on Heraldry', *The Antiquaries Journal*, xxxiii (1933).
LOOMIS, R. S., 'Arthurian Influences on Sport and Spectacle', *Arthurian Literature of the Middle Ages* (Clarendon Press, 1959), 553–9.
MCFARLANE, K. B., 'Parliament and Bastard Feudalism', *T.R.H.S.* (1944), 53–73.
—— *The Wars of the Roses* (Ralegh Lecture to the British Academy, 1964).
MCKISACK, M., *The Fourteenth Century* (Oxford, 1959).
Magdalen College, Oxford, Oxon. Charter No. 631.
MAITLAND, F. W., *Memoranda de Parliamento* (R.S. 1893).
MANN, SIR JAMES, *Arms and Armour in England* (H.M.S.O., 1960).
MARTIN, C., 'Walter Burley' in *Oxford Studies presented to Daniel Callus* (O.H.S., N.S. xvi, 1964).
MIDGLEY, L. M., *Ministers' Accounts of the Earldom of Cornwall, 1296–97*, 2 vols. (Camden Soc. 1942, 1945).
MOOR, the Rev. C., *Knights of Edward I*, 5 vols. (Harleian Soc., 1929–35).

LIST OF WORKS CITED

MURIMUTH, ADAM, *Continuatio Chronicarum* (1303–47), ed. E. M. Thompson (R.S. 1889).
NICHOLSON, RANALD, *Edward III and the Scots* (Oxford, 1965).
NICOLAS, Sir NICHOLAS HARRIS, *A Roll of Arms compiled in the reign of Edward III, 1337–40* (London, William Pickering, 1829).
PALGRAVE, F., *Documents relating to Scotland* (1832).
PARKER, J. H., 'Licences for Crenellation', *The Gentleman's Magazine* (N.S., 1856).
PATERSON, Lt.-Col. DANIEL, *Roads*, ed. Edward Mogg (18th edn., 1826).
Parliamentary Writs and Writs of Military Summons, ed. Sir F. Palgrave (Rec. Commission, 1827–34).
The Percy Chartulary, vol. 117, ed. M. T. Martin (Surtees Soc., 1909).
PLUCKNETT, T. F. T., *Statutes and their Interpretation in the First Half of the Fourteenth Century* (Cambridge, 1922).
—— on 'Parliament' in *The English Government at Work*, ed. Willard and others, q.v.
—— 'The Rise of the English State Trial', *Politica*, ii (1937).
POLLARD, A. F., *The Evolution of Parliament* (1926).
Polychronicon Ranulphi Higden, ed. C. Babington (R.S., 1869), vol. 2.
POWELL, E., *The Rising in East Anglia* (Cambridge, 1896).
POWER, EILEEN, *The Wool Trade in English Medieval History* (Oxford, 1941).
POWICKE, F. M., *The Thirteenth Century* (Oxford, 1953).
—— *Medieval England* (Home University Library).
PRINCE, A. E., 'The Strength of English Armies in the Reign of Edward III', *E.H.R.* xlvi (1931).
PUTNAM, BERTHA, *William Shareshull* (Cambridge, 1950).
—— 'The Transformation of the Keepers of the Peace to Justices of the Peace, 1327–80', *T.R.H.S.*, 4th ser., xii. 19–48.
RAINE, JAMES, *Historie Dunelmensis Scriptores Tres* (Surtees Soc., 1839).
RAMSAY, Sir JAMES, *The Dawn of the Constitution* (1908).
READING, JOHN OF, *Chronica*, ed. James Tait (Manchester, 1914).
Return of the Name of every member of the Lower House of Parliament, 1213–1874 (H.M.S.O., 1877 and 1878).
Robert of Gloucester's Chronicle (R.S. 1887).
Robert of Brunne's Chronicle (R.S. 1887).

ROBERTS, GLYN, 'Wales and England', *Welsh History Review*, i, No. 4 (1963).
RUSSELL, JOSIAH COX, *British Medieval Population* (1948).
SALTER, H. E., *The Boarstall Chartulary* (O.H.S. 1930).
SAYLES, G. O., 'Medieval Judges as Legal Consultants', *Law Quarterly Review* (1940), 247–54.
The Scrope and Grosvenor Controversy, ed. in 2 vols. by Henry Nicolas [Sir Nicholas Harris Nicolas] (London, 1832).
Select Passages from Bracton and Azo (Selden Soc.), ed. F. W. Maitland, 1895.
SHERBORNE, J. W., 'Indentured Retinues and the English Expeditions to France', *E.H.R.* (1964), 718–46.
SMITH, W. J., 'The "Revolt" of William de Somerton', *E.H.R.* lxix (1954), 76–83.
STONES, E. L. G., 'The Folevilles of Ashby Foleville and their Associates in Crime', *T.R.H.S.* (1957), 117–36.
—— 'Geoffrey Le Scrope (*c.* 1285–1340), Chief Justice of the King's Bench', *E.H.R.* (1952), lxix. 1–17.
STUBBS, W., *The Constitutional History of England*, 3 vols. (Oxford 1874–8).
—— *Select Charters*, 9th edn. rev. by H. W. C. Davis (1925).
TAYLOR, JOHN, *The Universal Chronicle of Ranulf Higden* (Clarendon Press, 1966).
TIPPING, H. A., *English Homes*, Period I (1066–1487) (London, 1921–37).
TOUT, T. F., *Chapters in English Administrative History*, 6 vols. (Manchester, 1923–35).
—— *Collected Papers*, 3 vols. (Manchester 1932).
TUPPING, H., *South Lancashire in the Reign of Edward II* (Chetham Soc., 1949).
Victoria County History.
WAGNER, Sir A., *Catalogue of English Medieval Rolls of Arms* (Soc. of Antiquaries, 1950).
—— *Heralds and Heraldry* (Clarendon Press, 2nd edn. 1956).
WOOD, MARGARET, *The English Medieval House, 1066–1540* (Country Life Publications, 1965).
WOOD-LEGH, 'The Knights' attendance in the Parliaments of Edward III', *E.H.R.* (1930) xlv. 398–413.
—— 'Sheriffs, Lawyers, and Belted Knights in the Parliaments of Edward I', *E.H.R.* (1931) xlvi. 372–88.

INDEX

Admiralty, Court of, 133.
Algeciras, 116.
Alton, Sir William, 142 n. 2.
Alverton, Mr. John, 127.
Ambrosden, co. Oxon., 123.
Andronicus, Emperor of Constantinople, 155.
—, —, his son Michael, 155.
Angus, Earl of, arms of, 112.
Appleby Castle, co. Westmorland, 34.
Ap Thomas, Sir Rhys, I, 115.
—, —, II, K.G., 115.
—, —, his great tournament, 115 n. 2.
Aquitaine, Duchy of, 125.
archers, mounted, 139.
archives, county, 33.
Argentine (Poitou); descent of the family of, 154 n. 1.
—, Giles de (d. 1314), 41, App. II, 154–5.
armies, organization of in the 14th century, 138–40.
armigeri in 1324, 5, 19.
—, forbidden to tourney, 141.
—, in 15th century, 6, 142 n. 3.
Arms, coats of, attached to dignities, 88.
arms, license to alienate, 136.
—, logical arrangement of charges in Cotgrave's Ordinary, 99.
—, Statute of, 148.
Arundel lions, 112.
—, Richard, Earl of, 152.
Ashmole Role 15A, 89, 96, 97, and n. 5, 98.
—, linked with Cotgrave's Ordinary, 98.
Ashridge, Bonhommes at, 122.
Asthall, co. Oxon., 123.
d'Aubigny, Ellis, 152.
Audley, arms of, 112.
—, Hugh de, 99.
—, Sir or Lord James, 128 n. 5, 135, 139 n. 1.

Aumale, William de Fortibus, Earl of (d. 1260), 88.
—, Isabella his wife, 88.

Bacheleria of 1259, 48, 71, 81.
Bacon, Francis, cited, 1.
Badlesmere, Bartholomew de, 80.
Baldock, Ralph, Bp. of London, Wardrobe ordinances of, 81.
Ball, John, 1, 4, 6, 7, 14.
Balliol, Edward, coronation of (1332), 97, 120.
—, does homage, at Newcastle, 97, 106.
—, leaves Scotland, 110.
— Roll (1334), 89, 96, 97, 120–1.
—, painted on the dorso of Cook's Ordinary (and therefore *c.* 1338–9), 120.
Bampton, co. Oxon., 126.
Banastre, Adam, 31.
Banbury, Sir Thomas de, 39.
bannerets and baronets, 5.
—, numbers of, 80.
—, ratio of to knights, 139.
Bannockburn, 141 and n. 4, 155.
Bardi–Peruzzi débâcle, 137.
Bardolf, Sir John, cadet of Bardolf family of Wormegay, co. Norf., 47.
Barford St. Michael, co. Oxon., 128 n. 4.
baronets and bannerets, 5.
baronial councils, statute of Richard II against, 129. *See also* Black Prince.
Barton Abbey, co. Oxon., 130 n. 1.
— Odonis, co. Oxon., 130 n. 1.
Basset, William, 125.
bastardy, 4.
Beauchamp, Guy, Earl of Warwick, 12.
—, Humphrey, M.P., 65.
—, Ralph de, 60.
—, Thomas de, Earl of Warwick (1335), 86 n. 3, 104.

INDEX

Beaumont of Devon, 99.
—, Henry de, 80.
—, John de, 144.
—, Louis (al. Lewis) de, Bp. of Durham (1317–33), 2, 8.
Beckley, oak-woods at, 126.
Bedford, Lancaster's demonstration at, 90.
Bedfordshire M.P.s. (1327–36), 51.
beds, bequeathed by will, 38.
le Bel, Jean, 100, 101.
Bensington, co. Oxon., 122, 135.
Benson, co. Oxon., court of the $4\frac{1}{2}$ hundreds of, 126.
Benstead (Benstede), John, 8, 10, 11, 36.
Bereford, Sir Edmund de, and his three sisters, 128 n. 5.
Bergh, Thomas atte, 52.
Berkeley Castle, Edward II at, guarded by his own household officials, 80, 106.
Berkhamsted, 124.
—, the beeches at, 126.
Bertram, 87.
Berwick, homages done at (1334), 120.
Bigod, Roger, the Earl Marshal, 124.
Bikenor, Sir Robert de, M.P., 72 n. 2.
Bittlesden Priory, 123.
Black Death, the, 3, 94 and n. 2, 106.
Black Prince, the, 25, 68, 71, 107, 135, 144, 145, 146, 147, 148.
—, his generosity, 139, 140.
—, buys ostrich feathers, 145 n. 1.
—, borrows £10 from his herald, 148.
—, his appanage, 125 ff.
—, his lavish grants after Poitiers, 127.
—, conciliar activity on his estates, 128.
—, his Exchequer, Wardrobe, and Council at Westminster, 125.
—, his feodary, 125.
—, his escheator, 125.
—, his King of Arms, 148.
—, lavish to minstrels, heralds, and friars, 148.
Bocking, Sir Ralph, M.P. for Suff. twenty-two times, 48, 59, 70.

Bodrigan, Sir Odo de, 72 n. 2.
Bohun family, as patrons of literature, 12 and n. 2. See also Hereford, Northampton.
—, Humphrey de, Earl of Hereford (in 1300), 151.
—, — (in 1304), 153.
—, William de, Earl of Northampton (cr. 1337), 120, 144.
Boneville family, of Shute, co. Somerset, M.P.s, 67.
Bordesley, Cistercian abbey, co. Worcs., 12.
Boroughbridge Roll of Arms (1322), 34, 76–80.
—, the battle of, 76–7.
Bothwell Castle, 120.
Bottisham, co. Camb., 154.
Boulton, Thomas de, 138.
Bourchier, Robert, 12.
Brabant, embassy to (1284), 73.
Brackley, co. Northants., tournament at (1313), 141 n. 4.
— Priory, 123.
Bradston, Lord, 9 n. 1.
Bray, Mr. Henry de, 83 n. 2.
Bren, Llewellyn, 31.
Breton prisoners, 148.
Briançon, Joan de, 73.
Bridlington, John of, 105.
— Priory, 40 n. 1.
Brittany, Duke of (1375), 139.
Britton, 87.
Brotherton, Thomas de (d. 1338), 84, 86.
Bruce, David, 102.
—, —, Joan his wife, 102.
Bruces, the (1334), 106.
Bruiant, Le Roi, the Earl of Lancaster's herald king (1322), 76.
Buckingham's expedition (1380), 139.
Bullock-Davies, Mrs. C., 93 n. 2.
Burdet, Robert, M.P., 66.
Burgh, Elizabeth de, 107.
—, Hubert de, 73.
—, co. Kent, 119.
Burgherssh, Bartholomew, the son, 125, 127.
Burke, Edmund, cited, 100.

INDEX

Burley, Simon, 38.
Burne, Colonel A. H., cited, 25.
Burnell, Nicholas, Lord, 135–6.
—, Robert, 44.
Burton-on-Trent, 39.
Bury, Richard de, 39.
—, —, and the *coup d'état* of 1330, 90.
—, —, mission to France (1336), 93.
—, —, his quality as ambassador, 93.
Butler, James, Duke of Ormonde, 84.
Buzones, 2–3, 42, 68.

cadency, marks of, 4.
Caen, storm of (1346), 137.
Caerlaverock Castle, the muster at, 150–1.
— —, events following the capture of, 151.
— poem, 33.
Caernarvon Castle, 33.
Caernarvon, the Record of, 94 n. 2.
Calais, siege of, 136.
Calendars of Close Rolls, 55.
Cam, Professor H., on 14th-century M.P.s, 53 ff.
Camden, William, confuses two battles, 152 n. 3.
Canterbury, Holy Trinity Priory at, 39.
Carlisle Herald, 79, 101, 105.
— Roll, 89, 96, 98, 101–4, 113.
Carmarthen, county court of, 34.
—, the sheriff's office at, 115.
—, Franciscans of, 115.
—, Grey Friars of, 115.
castles, 32 ff.
—, cost of building, 36.
—, in Gascony, 36 n. 1.
—, local distribution of, 37.
—, as local treasuries, 78 and n. 2.
Cavendish, Sir John, 38.
Chamber estates, 81.
champions, hereditary, of the Dukes of Normandy, 88.
Champvent, Peter de, 44.
Chancery, clerks of the, 43 ff.
Chandos, Sir John, 72 n. 2.
Charney Basset, co. Berks., 34.

Chaucer, Geoffrey, 23–4, 39, 62, 135, 149.
—, Sir Thomas, 129 n. 6.
Chauvency in Flanders, tournament at (1285), 79.
Cheapside, tournament at, 143.
Cherleton, John, of Shropshire, 95.
Cheshire, churches in (named), 134 n. 3.
Chester, 91 n. 3, 125.
—, Earls of, 134.
— Castle, Welsh hostages in, 78.
Chiltern hundreds, the, 122, 126.
chivalers, 19, 58.
Chivalry, High Court of, 133.
—, conscious, 100.
Christ Church, Canterbury, retains counsel, 130 n. 4.
Clare family, history of (1262–1314), 108–9. See Gloucester.
—, Gilbert de, last of his line (d. 1314), 107.
—, Richard de, 108.
—, arms of, 108.
—, co. Suffolk, 107.
Clarence, Lionel, Duke of, (created 1362), 107.
—, formerly Lionel of Antwerp, 107 n. 1.
—, Thomas of Lancaster, Duke of (1411–22), 84.
Clarenceux (Clarincell) Andrew, 97, 106, 107–9.
—, antedates Lionel of Clarence, 107 n. 1.
—, takes his title from Clare in Suffolk, *caput* of the Gloucester honour of Clare, 107
Clifford, Mr. Richard de, 83 n. 2.
—, Sir (or Lord) Robert of Clifford Castle, co. Heref. [*see* my *History and Heraldry*, passim].
—, Lord Roger (1322), 80.
Clifton, Sir Gervase, 135.
Clinton, William de, Constable of Dover and Warden of the Cinque Ports, 93, 98. *See* Huntingdon.
Cobham, John de, 38.
Cobham, Reginald, 137.

INDEX

Cobham, Thomas de, 130 n. 4.
Cokeyne, John, M.P. for co. Derby. twelve times, 59.
Coleville of Cambridgeshire, 99.
Collins's Roll, 119.
Columbers, Matthew de, 27–8.
commilitones, 41.
Commons, composition of the, 52.
Constable of England, perquisites of the, 86.
—, at musters, 150.
—, powers of, 133.
—, in 1417, 84.
—, *see also* Marshal.
Constables of Flamborough, co. Yorks., 36.
contracts to raise troops, 137–8.
Cooke, Sir Robert, Clarenceux, 115.
Cooke's Ordinary, 9, 34, 89, 95, 98, 105, 111–18.
Corbet family, 60.
—, Thomas, M.P., 59.
Cornishmen, 99.
Cornwall, Richard, Earl of (d. 1272), 121, 125.
—, —, Edmund (d. 1300), 121.
—, —, the Black Prince as, 121.
—, made a duchy (1337), 121–2.
Coroners, 49–52.
Corrodars, civil servants as, 38–40.
Costessy, co. Norf., 119.
Cotesford, Sir Roger de, 128 n. 2.
Cotgrave's Ordinary, 89, 98.
— —, its great importance, 111–14.
Cotton, William, of Cotton by Chester, 136.
Council, Clerk of the, 44.
country houses, 34–8.
Courtenay, Hugh, the elder, Earl of Devon, 90–1.
—, Hugh, 97 n. 5.
Coventry, John of, 38, 129 n. 6.
Craon, Maurice de, 152.
Crawthorne, Matthew de, M.P., 66 n. 1.
Crécy, battle of, 9, 25, 94, 132, 135.
—, —, no roll for, 101.
Cree, R., in Scotland, 151.
Creetown, 151.

crenellation, 31, 34–8.
Crispin, Miles, 122.
Croft, Sir Hugh, gallant M.P. for Salop, 59.
crosses, not the earliest form of charges, 113.
Crowmarsh Giffard, co. Oxon., 126.

Dale, Sir Dietrich Van, 24.
Dammartin, Charles, Count of, 140.
Damory, Roger, 133.
Daniel, Sir John, 148 and n. 1.
Delves, Richard, of Delves Hall, co. Staffs. (d. 1369), 139 n. 1.
—, Sir John, his son, 139 n. 1.
Derby, Earl of, lions passant, 112.
—, —, Henry, 137, 142.
Despenser, Hugh le, the elder, Earl of Winchester, (1322–6), 135.
—, —, the younger, M.P., 63.
—, other M.P.s of this name and their arms, 63 and nn. 4, 5.
—, Philip, 146.
D'Eyncourt, Edmund, 136.
Disinherited, the (1267), 108.
Doget, Stephen, 104 n. 1.
d'Oilly, Robert, 122.
—, —, Matilda his daughter, 122.
Dorchester, co. Oxon., 128.
Douglas, Sir William of Liddesdale, 116.
Dover, constables of, 43 n. 2.
Drakensford, John de, the younger, 10 n. 3, 91 n. 3.
Droxford, John de, 8, 10–11 and nn.
Duchayn, Nicholas, 148.
Dugdale, Sir William, 113.
Dunstable tournament (1334), retinues at, 84.
— —, Roll of, 89, 96, 97, 142 n. 2.
—, tournaments at, 120, 142, 143, 144.
Durham, 91 n. 3.
Dymoke, John, 88.

Edward I, 9.
—, at Blyth in 1254, 89.
—, at Twynham, 151.

INDEX

— and Edward III, 92, 93.
—, no real affection for knights and burgesses, 55.
Edward II, as Prince of Wales, 95.
—, unusual activity in 1324, 17.
—, at Berkeley Castle, 72 n. 1.
Edward III, King of England, knighted and crowned, 89.
—, his first *chevauchée*.
—, assumption of power (October 1330), 90.
—, initiates *querele* into local government, 90.
—, creation of three earldoms, 90.
—, mercantilist policy, 91, 37.
—, sumptuary legislation, 91.
—, his character, 91, 137.
—, as a successful planner and quartermaster, 92–3.
—, better served than Edward I, 93.
—, his Welsh followers, 95.
—, financial policy, 100.
—, his choice of entertainments, 106.
—, his great triumphs, 114.
—, his generals, 137.
—, tourneys in person, 144, 145 n. 1, 147.
—, swears to renew the Round Table of Arthur, 147.
Edwards, Professor Sir Goronwy, cited, 59 n. 2, 74.
Elsefield, Sir Gilbert de, 128 n. 5.
English language, use of, 12–13.
Erd or Erthe (Scotland), 103.
escheators, importance and functions of, 83 and nn. 1, 2.
esquiers, 19, 141 n. 4.
— in tournaments, 141 n. 4.
Etchingham (*al.* Echingham), William de, 21.
Eu, Count of, 137.
Evesham, battle of, no roll for, 101.
Ewelme, half-hundred of, co. Oxon., 129 n. 6.
Exchequer, reforms at (1323–4), 81.
Eye, Philip of, 39.

Falkirk, battle of, 101, 103, 133 n. 5.

faux escutcheon, 87.
Fécamp Abbey, 39.
fencible men, 129 n. 6.
feodary, duties of a, 127.
Fitz-Warin, Fulk, 99.
Flanders and Brabant, diplomatic relations with, 80.
Fletcher, Miss Margery, on Bedfordshire M.P.s, 51.
Foleville family, 31.
Fontenay, barony of, 88.
Fors, William de, de Vivonia, 27.
Forz, Isabella de, death of, 90. *See also* Isabella, the Countess.
Foxle, John and Thomas, M.P.s for Berks., 57 n. 3.
France, war against, decided upon on or before 6 August 1336 (*not* 1337), 92.
franklins, 4 ff., 19, 23 ff.
— as M.P.s, 57.
— in Chaucer, 57.
Fraser, Simon, 73.
Fraunk, William, one of Edward III's quartermasters, 92.
Frederick, King of Sicily, 155.
French Revolution, 131.
Freville family, 88.
Froissart, poet, herald-painter, and chronicler, 100, 101, 106.
—, cited (*s.a.* 1390), 148.
Fychan, Ednyfed, 94.

Gacelyn, Sir Edmund, M.P., 57.
Galloway Roll of Arms (1300), 151–2.
Garter, inauguration of the Order of the, 146–7.
— King of Arms (1415), 147.
—, Knights of the, 41.
Gascelyn family, 60.
Gascony, Ordinances for, 81.
Gaunt, John of, 71, 132, 138 n. 6.
—, —, marries Blanche of Lancaster, 145.
Gaveston, Piers, 143.
Genoa, *podestà* of, 155.
gentlemen, definitions of, 4.
—, men of law not, 130. *See also* Ball, Adam.

INDEX

Gervays, George, of Wycombe, yeoman and escheator, 125.
Gloucester Cathedral, 9.
— chevronels, 112.
— earldom, break-up of (1314), 107.
—, Gilbert (the Red) de Clare, Earl of, 108, 109.
—, Gilbert, the last Earl (d. 1314), 109.
—, —, at Dunstable tournament (1310), 109.
Glover's Roll, 34.
Goldington, William de, M.P., 66 n. 2.
Gravesend, co. Kent, 119.
Grey, John de, M.P., 65.
—, Lord of Powys, 95.
—, Sir Thomas, of Heton, 154.
Grosvenor, Robert, 133.
—, —, his father, 134 n. 3.
—, —, supporters of, in Wales and Cheshire, 135.
Gurney, Lord Thomas, 72 n. 1.
—, —, Steward of the Royal Household (1330), 71.

Hailes Abbey, co. Glos., 122.
Hainault, the Count of, 144.
Halidon Hill, battle of, 97, 100, 120, 135.
Hamilton, William de, 44.
Harclay, Sir Andrew, Earl of Carlisle (1322), traitor, 77.
Harlech Castle, 94.
Haydok family, M.P.s, 65.
Haye, John de la, M.P., 66.
Hearst, Mr. Randolph, 35 n. 3.
Hemingburgh Rectory, co. Yorks., 11.
Hengham, Ralph de, 130 n. 4.
Henley-on-Thames, co. Oxon., 123.
Henry of Luxemburg, 154.
Henry I, 'raised [men] from the dust', 90.
heraldic treatise, a little, 96.
Herald-painter of Carlisle Roll, 104 and n. 1.
Herald-painters in 14th and 15th centuries, 104 n. 1.
Heralds, appointment of, 85.
— named in Black Prince's *Register*, 148 n. 4.

—, Le Roy Aquitaigne, 136.
—, Le Roy Vaillant, 136.
— *See also* Bruiant, Carlisle, Lancaster.
Hereford, the Earl of (d. 1322), 77.
—, Humphrey de Bohun IX, Earl of, Constable of England (d. 1336), 102, 104, 105.
—, — X (d. 1373), 105.
—, —, his aunt Eleanor, 105.
Hertford, tournament at (Sept. 1342), 120.
Hever, 35 n. 1.
Higden, Ranulf, 14.
Holland, Thomas de (d. 1372), becomes 'a millionaire', 137.
Hood, Robin, 31, 49.
Horn, Andrew (d. 1329), 87.
Hospital, the Master of the, 155.
Huddleston, Richard de, le fils, 152.
Hungerford, Sir Thomas, M.P. and Speaker, 68.
Hunnisett, Mr. R. F., on *The Medieval Coroner*, 2, 51 ff.
Huntingdon (Clinton), earldom of created, 90.
—, had he a herald?, 97 n. 5.

indexes, in 16th and 17th centuries, 113.
inescutcheons, increased use of, 87.
—, examples from Glover's Roll and Boroughbridge Roll, 87.
Ingleby, Sir Thomas, 35 n. 3.
Ipsden, co. Oxon., 125.
Isabella, the Countess, 127. *See* Aumale
— of France, Queen of England, 1, 16, 31.
—, —, and Mortimer, 81, 82.
—, —, invades England (1326), 31.
—, —, as the Queen Mother, 145.
— of Hainault, Queen of England, 94, 143.

Jenyns, William, his Ordinary, 89, 112.
—, Thomas, 112.
John of Brittany, Earl of Richmond (cr. 1306), 145 n. 1, 152.
Jorz family, as local gangsters, 49–51.

INDEX

Judges, as knights, 132.
judicial combat, 141 n. 3.
—, scandals of 1289 and 1340, 132 n. 1.
Juliers, William V, Count of, 101 and n. 3.

Keith, Robert, Marshal of Scotland, 151.
Kelkfeld de Escoce, 115.
Kendal family, 42–6.
—, Hugh de (d. 1297), as chancery clerk and household clerk, 43–4.
—, Hugh as *clericus de consilio*, 44.
Kendale, Sir Edmund de, of co. Rutland, 136–7.
Kenilworth Castle, 34, 37.
Kent, Earl of, youngest son of Edward I, 141–2.
—, —, execution of, 84, 143.
—, rebels in (1381), 131.
King, Gregory, demographer and Lancaster Herald, 3, 5, 6 n. 1, 7.
Kingsford, C. L., cited, 129.
Kirby Knole, co. Yorks., 35.
Kirkbride, Richard of, 152.
Knights, amalgamation in war with squires, 2.
—, King's, 42.
—, mass knighting in 1324, 17–18.
—, distraint of knighthood, 17 n. 1, 91 and n. 3, 106.
— ratio of, to men-at-arms, 139.
— in retainder, 41 n. 2.
— of the shire, corruption and payment of, 61–3 and n. 1.
—, relation with burgesses, 64–5.
— of the Swan, 41.
— local, 48 ff.
—, —, as coroners and verderers, 49 ff.
—, —, hanker after local office, 49.
—, —, as 14th-century M.P.s, 52 ff.

Lancaster, Henry of, in 1328–9, 84, 90.
—, Henry and Thomas of, 152.
—, Henry of Grosmont, Earl of, Earl of Derby, 1337, 116.
—, —, Duke of Lancaster, 1351, 116.

—, —, lands in Kidwelly and Monmouth, 116.
—, —, Keeper of castle, town and county of Carmarthen (1342), 116.
—, —, as a jouster, 116.
—, —, inherited and rebuilt the Savoy, 117.
—, —, in France, 116–17.
—, —, his descent, 118.
—, Thomas Earl of, defeated at Boroughbridge (1322), 76.
—, —, tried and beheaded, 77.
—, —, his character, 78, 80.
—, —, Henry his brother, 80.
—, Duke of, 60, 139.
—, Earl of, in 1337–8, 21.
— Herald (in 1322 ?), 79.
— —, in 1346, 136.
Langford family, co. Hants, 46.
— —, John, Nicholas, and William, 46.
Langton, John, chancellor (1292–1302), 44 and n. 5.
—, Walter, 73–4.
Lapsley, Gaillard, cited, 3.
Lascelles, Roger de, 35.
Latimer, Lord (1322), 80.
Laton, Sir John, 134.
—, Sir Robert, 5, 23.
Lavagna, the Count of, 155.
lawyers, professional, found county families, 129.
Leicester, Peter de, 38.
Lennox, Earl (Patrick) of, and his son, 152.
Leukenore, John de, the Earl Marshal's deputy at court in 1337, 85 n. 2.
Leyburne, Roger, in Kent, 36.
Liber Quotidianus Garderobae Regis, 152 n. 2.
Limbergh, Tideman de, 125.
Lincoln, Bp. of, dispute with Black Prince, 128.
—, Earl of, 133 n. 3.
—, tournaments at, 147 and n. 1.
Lindsay, 87.
lion or leopard, 87 and n. 4 (Ludlow, Tregoz).

Lisle estates, 137.
Little Chesterford, co. Essex, 34.
Little Wenham Hall, co. Suff., 34.
Llewelyn the Great, and his descendants, 95.
Llwyd, Sir Griffith, 94.
London, Cripplegate, 119.
—, Smithfield, the Charter-house, 94.
Longuevill, Sir John de, M.P., on Bracton, 65.
Louth, Mr. William de, keeper of the Wardrobe, 44.
Lovel, John, Lord of Titchmarsh, 136.
Lovetot, Sir John (d. 1305), and his family, 73.
Lucy, Sir Thomas de, M.P., 71.
— Sir William de, M.P., 71.
Ludlow, Margaret, 88.
Lundy Island, 72 n. 2.
Luton, co. Beds., jousts at, 141 n. 2.
Lutterworth, co. Leics., 88.

McFarlane, Mr. K. B. F., on *Parliament and Bastard Feudalism*, 59 n. 3, 84.
McKisack, Professor M., *The Fourteenth Century*, 53 n. 2, 54, 89.
Magdalen College, Oxford, 34.
Malmesbury, the Monk of, 39–40, 81.
— Abbey, corrodars at, 39, 40 n. 1.
Maltravers (Mautravers), family, 71, 72 and n. 1., 128 n. 5.
—, Sir John, 32, 119.
Mandeville, Sir John, 13.
manor houses, 34–8.
Mansel, John, 45 n. 2.
Manuscripts: Cambridge, FitzWilliam Museum MS. 324 (Carlisle Role), 105.
—, London, Brit. Mus. Add. MS. 43650 (Wardrobe account, 1332), 97 n. 2.
—, —, — Cott. MS. Nero C. viii, 104.
—, —, — Cott. MS. Caligula A. xviii. The PRA, Caerlaverock poem on the spy Turberville, 75.
—, —, — Cott. MS. Nero D. vi, 86.

—, —, — Egerton MS. Add. 2850, 76.
—, —, Coll. of Arms MS. 14, 152.
—, —, P.R.O. E 101/8/26, 152 n. 2.
—, —, — E 101/387/9 (counter roll of Wardrobe, 1332), 97 n. 2.
—, —, — Min. Acct. 961/6, 958/19, 123 nn. 2, 3.
—, Oxford, Bod. Lib. Ashm. roll 15A., 4 nn. 1, 2.
—, —, — MS. Ashmole 804 (Powell's Roll), 118, 119.
—, —, Magd. Coll. ch. no. 631 (Woodstock 9), 123.
—, Wales, U.C.N.W. Bangor, The Record of Caernarvon, 94 n. 2.
Mapledurham Gurney, manor of, co. Berks., 47–8.
March, Mr. William de, controller of the wardrobe, 44.
Marche, de la, Thomas, 141 n. 3.
Mare, Peter de la, M.P. and Speaker, 68.
Mareschal, John le, M.P., 65.
Marmion, Amice, 88 n. 3.
—, Manasser, 88 n. 3.
—, Philip, 88.
—, Robert, 88.
Marshal, the Earl, his perquisites, 85, 86.
—, —, his herald, 86 n. 2.
—, —, his powers, 133.
—, —, demoted in 1377, 71.
—, the Earl Marshal's deputy, values the horses and makes horse-inventories, 150.
—, —, collects contracts of service, 150.
Marshal, William the, 133.
Martel, William, 138 n. 2.
Mauny, Walter (in 1332), 90.
—, —, as a quartermaster, 92.
—, —, sheriff of Merioneth, 93, 94.
—, —, career, 94, 137.
—, —, as a wealthy baron, 137.
Mautravers, *see* Maltravers.
Maxwell, Sir Eustace, 102.
Melksop, William, 141 n. 2.
Melton, William, treasurer of England (1325), 81.

INDEX

men-at-arms (1334), 139.
Middleton, Gilbert de, 31.
miles literatus, 2.
'Mirror of Justices', 87.
Modus tenendi Parliamentum, 87.
Moleyns, John de, keeper of lands assigned to the Chamber (1337), 8.
Monchesney, 87.
Montague, Simon de (in 1300), 152.
—, — (October 1330), 90.
— (Montacute), William de, Earl of Salisbury (cr. 1337), 21, 85, 120.
— arms, 112.
Montferrat, the Marquess of, 155.
Montfort, Peter de, of Beaudesert, 119.
Monthermer eagles, 112.
—, Ralph, Earl of Gloucester, 152.
Morby [possibly for Morley], Richard de, M.P., 66 n. 2.
Morley, Sir Robert (Lord), 136, 144.
—, Thomas, Lord, 136.
Mortimer, the inescutcheon, 87.
—, Constantine de, of Sculton, co. Norf., 36, 56.
—, Edmund, Earl of March, 71.
—, Roger, 1, 16.
—, —, his treaty with the Scots, 90.
—, —, attack on, at Nottingham Castle, 119.
—, —, marriage of his daughter, 142.
—, —, execution of, 143.
Morys (Moriz), Sir John, M.P. for borough and shire of Cambridge, 60.
Munpellers, Henry de, 38.
muster, a great, in 1324, 16.
Muster rolls, their limitations as historical evidence, 150.

Najera, battle of, 132.
nationalism, 13.
Neath Castle in Glamorgan, 78 n. 2.
Nefyn (1284), 141 n. 1, 145.
Neville, Ralph, 49 n. 1.
Neville's Cross, battle of, 132.
Newcastle-on-Tyne, Edward III at (1334), 106.
Newton Stewart, in Scotland, 151.

Nith, River, 152.
Norroy, Andrew Rex, 109 and n. 2.
Northampton, Michael of, 124.
— (Bohun), earldom of created, 90.
—, the Earl of as one of Edward III's generals, 137.
—, in tourney, 144.
—, *see* Bohun.
— Castle, 76.
—, parliament of (1328), 90.
—, Statute of (1328), 143.
—, tournament at (1323), 142.
—, Treaty of (1328), 90, 105.
Northumberland, knights in, 20.
Norwich, John of, Admiral of the North Sea fleet, 92.
—, the Shirehous, 33.
Nottingham, Edward III at, 102.
— Castle, 37.

Oddyngseles, Sir John de, 30 n. 3.
Ordinances of 1311, revocation of, 81.
Orford, co. Suff., 119.
Ormesby, John de, M.P. for Norfolk, 56.
Oseney Abbey, 39.
— —, Abbot of, 123.
—, North, co. Oxon., 123.
Oxford, Earl of, arms, 112.
—, —, in 1388, 38.
— Castle, 33.
—, Priory of St. Frideswide, 123.
— University, Ashmolean Museum, 35 n. 3.
Oxfordshire, M.P.s for, 57.
—, under sheriff's account, 129 n. 6.

Panfletus, 87.
Paris, Matthew, cited, 89.
Parker, J. H., on *Domestic Architecture*, 35–6.
Parliament, relation of the Commons to the Lords, 67–9.
—, position of the Speaker, 68–9, 70.
—, influence of King and King's Knights on, 71–2.
—, King's bannerets and judges in the Lords, 72.

Parliament (*cont.*)
— of York (2 May 1322), Lincoln (Sept. 1327), 56; of 1339, 1350, 1360, 1368, 1369, 1376 (the Good Parliament), 48, 59, 71.
—, re-election of M.P.s, 58, 59.
— rigging of elections, 60–1.
—, *valetti*, yeomen, or franklins in, 60–1.
—, burgesses, 60.
Parliamentary Roll of Arms (PRA), 16, 112.
—, additions to, in the Lancastrian interest, 83–5.
Peasants' Revolt, 14.
Pecché, Gilbert, royalist, 80.
Pecham, John, Abp. of Canterbury, 95.
Pedro, Don, 132.
Pembroke, Earl of, his manor of Bampton, 126, 144.
Penchester, Sir Stephen de, 34, 35 n. 1.
Penmynydd in Angelsey, home of the Tudors, 96.
Penshurst, co. Sussex, 34.
Percy, Lord Henry, his life retainer from the Crown (1331), 138.
—, —, his contract with Edward Balliol (1333), 138.
Perers, Sir Richard, Kt., six times M.P. for Herts., 58.
—, —, in Lancaster's retinue at first Dunstable tournament, 58 n. 3.
Perth, Edward III at, 103.
Peyton, John de, 119.
Philip of Valois, King of France, 93.
Philippa, of Hainault, Queen of England, 145.
Phillipps, Sir Thomas, Bart., 115.
pilgrimages, 72 n. 2.
Pipardesclive, co. Wilts., 27.
Plucknett, Professor T. F. T., on Parliament, 51, 59 n. 4.
Poever, Over and Nether, co. Cheshire, 134 n. 3.
Poile, John de la, M.P., 65.
Poitiers, battle of, 25.
—, —, no roll for, 101.

Pole, Michael de la, ennobled, as Earl of Suffolk (1385), 90, 145.
poll-tax of 1381, 16.
Pomeroy estates, 137.
Pontefract ('Pomfret') Castle, 77.
Ponton, William de, 141 n. 2.
Pope, public letters to the, in 13th and 14th centuries, 54–5.
population, 15–16.
Powell's Roll, 89, 118–20.
Poywicke, Mr. William de, 130 n. 4.
Pulteney impeached, 145.
Purcell family, 130.

querelae of 1289–90 and 1330, 137.

Ragman Roll of 1296, 97.
Ramsay, Sir Alexander, of Dalhousie, 116.
—, Sir James, 97.
Ramsey Abbey, 38.
ransoms and spoils of war, 137–40.
Return of M.P.s, its deficiencies, 55–6, 57.
Rewley Abbey, co. Oxon., 122.
Rhodes, island of, 155.
Richard II, Welsh servants of, 95.
Richard, Earl of Cornwall (d. 1272), 121.
Richmond, liberty of, 133 n. 3.
Ridewere, Sir Robert de, 30 n. 3.
Ripley Castle, co. Yorks., 35 n. 3.
Rither, Sir John, 142 n. 2.
Rivers, Richard de, M.P., 65.
Roberts, Professor Glyn, 94, 96.
Roger of Chester, rector of Grappenhall, 148.
Rokele, Thomas de la, M.P., 65.
Ros, Margaret de, of Hamlake, 43.
Ross, Sir Thomas, of Kendale, 142.
Roubiry, Gilbert, 45 n. 3.
Round Tables at Bedford (1328) and Hereford, 142.
— —, meaning of, 146.
Round, J. H., 108, 114.
Rous, Sir John le, M.P., 66.
Roxburghe, tilt at (1341), 116.
Russell, Professor J. C., cited, 3.
Rye, sea-fight near, 132.

INDEX 173

St. Donat's Castle, co. Glam., 35 n. 3.
St. George, cult of, 144–5, 146 n. 2.
St. John, John de, 152 n. 2.
St. Valery, honour of, 122.
Say, Geoffrey de, a banneret of Kent (d. 1359), 92.
—, —, his life-contract (1349), 138.
Scalacronica, the, 154.
Scoteny, Walter de, 108.
Scotland, campaigns against, 89, 92–3, 96–7.
—, invasion of (1335), 101 ff.
Scottish invasion of Northumberland (1327), 106.
Scrivelsby, 88.
Scrope family, 36.
—, Geoffrey le, Knighted, 142 and n. 2.
—, —, of Masham (d. 1340), 132, 135.
—, Henry, his elder brother, 85, 130, 132, 133 n. 3.
—, —, Richard his son, 132–3, 134.
—, —, William, 133 n. 3.
—, Sir William, 142 n. 2.
Scrope-Grosvenor controversy, 5, 133–5, 142 n. 2.
Scutiferi, 19.
Seagrave, Lord, professional brawler, 80.
Secheville, John, of Kent, M.P., 65.
Secretarius Regis, 45.
Servat, William, Cahorsin merchant, 36.
Shakespeare, William, 38.
Shareshull, C. J., on Black Prince's council, 128.
—, his career, 130.
Sheriff, position of the, 54, 82.
—, —, helps to explain some Rolls of Arms, 82.
Sheriffs all changed (1340), 132 n. 1.
Sherwood Forest, 49.
Shields, the earliest, 87.
Smithfield, jousting for three days at (1343), 144.
—, 148.
Somerton, William de, 31.
Somervill, Philip de, M.P. for Staffs., and benefactor to Balliol College, 58.

Southwell, co. Notts., 142 n. 2.
Spigurnell, Sir Ralph, 125.
Squires, amalgamation in war with knights, 2, 4.
Stafford, Earl of (1373), 139.
Stanegrave, Robert de M.P., 66.
Stanhope (Stannow) Park, co. Northumberland, 89, 105, 142 n. 2.
Stannow, *see* Stanhope Park.
Stanton Harcourt, co. Oxon., 130.
Stapelton, Sir Miles de, 146.
Staple, the, at Calais, 91.
Stapledon, Walter, Bp. of Exeter, 81.
—, —, murdered (1326), 131.
Statuta, interpretation of, 64.
—, *Vetera Statuta* and *Nova Statuta*, 64.
Steeplebarton, co. Oxon., 130 n. 1.
Stephen, King of England (1235–54), his love of tournaments, 108.
Steward, treatise on the, 87.
Stillingfleet rectory, co. Yorks., 11.
Stirling Bridge, battle of (1297), 152 n. 3.
— Roll of Arms (1304), 152–3.
Stones, Professor E. L. G., cited, 130.
Stonor, Sir Thomas, 129 n. 6.
—, judge, on Black Prince's Council, 128.
— family, 129.
Stradling, Sir Peter, 35 n. 3.
Stratton, Adam de, 88.
—, Richard de, 126.
Stubbs, Bp. W., 39–40.
—, —, in error, 59.
Suffolk, Earl of, arms, 112.
—, —, as a general, 137.
—, —, in tournament, 144.
—, —, *see* Ufford.
Sully, Sir John, K.G., 135 and n. 3.
— of Iddesleigh, co. Devon, 135.
Sumptuary laws, 91 and n. 2.
surnames, use of, 13.
Swans, Feast of the (1306), 3.
Swynnerton, John de, M.P. for Staffs., 56.

Tamworth Castle, 88.
Tankerville, the Chamberlain of, 148 n. 1.

INDEX

Teirsaunte, John, a royal herald (1332–4), 86 n. 2.
Temple, the Master of the, 123.
tenant-farmers of Bensington, 125.
Thame, co. Oxon., 128.
Theseus, a referee, 149.
Thomas of Woodstock, Constable of England (1376–97), his rules for the tournament, 148.
Thorp, Sir William, 132 n. 1.
Tiptoft, Lord John, Earl of Worcester and Constable of England, 148.
Touchet, Mons., of Derbyshire, 99.
tournaments, prohibitions of (1310–17), 109, 141–2, 143.
—, unlicensed, under Edward II, 140 and n. 2, 141.
—, under Edward III, no longer prohibited, 140–9.
—, at Eltham, Smithfield, and Windsor, 141.
—, abroad, after 1312, 141.
—, at Guildford, Newmarket, and Dunstable, 142 n. 2.
—, Queen Isabella at, 143.
—, at Langley, Reading, and Dunstable, 143.
—, in Scotland, 143.
—, horses at, the prize of the victor, 144.
—, no casualties at (1342), 144.
—, at Windsor, 145–8.
—, at Eltham, 144 n. 1.
—, at Canterbury and Hereford, 144 n. 2.
—, nineteen held in 1348, 146.
—, rules for, 148 and n. 5.
Tower of London, the zoo, 87.
Trailbaston, 30.
Trailly, John, 140.
Trivet, Nicholas, 3 n. 3.
Trumwyme family, as M.Ps., 65.
Trussel, Sir William Kt., and M.P., 63 and nn. 2, 4, 5, 83 n. 2.
Tudors, origin of the, 96.
Turbervile, Payn, 31.
Turberville, Thomas, of Crickhowell, traitor, 74 ff.
—, Hugh, 74 and n.

Turbervilles, the Dorset and Glamorgan branches, 76 n. 1.
Tyes, Lord, professional brawler, 80.
— chevrons, 112.
Tynedale, Walter of, 20.

Ufford, Sir Robert, Earl of Suffolk (1337), 113, 119.
— family, 119.
— —, arms, 113, 120 n. 1.

valetti, 6, 19.
Valognes, Cecily de, 119.
Vaughan of Corsygedol, 94.
Verderers, 49 ff.
Verdon of Derbyshire, 99.
Vere, de, as Chamberlain, 28.
—, family long royalist, 80.
Visconti, Giovanni, 141 n. 2.
visitations, heraldic, 7.

Wagner, Sir A., 97 n. 5, 101, 102, 108, 114.
—, —, cited at length, 112.
Wales, Prince of, *see* Black Prince.
—, 125.
— sends twenty-four M.P.s to Westminster (1327), 94.
—, North, value of, 93.
—, Welsh gentry in the Middle Ages, 94.
—, Welsh society in the 14th century, 94–6.
Wallingford, honour of, 121–32.
—, —, court of the, 123, 125, 126.
—, —, —, encroaching on other courts, 126.
—, —, system of account in, 124.
—, tournament at (1307), 109.
Walton Ordinances, the, 93.
Walwayn, Mr. John, 39–40, 83 n. 2.
Warborough, co. Oxon., 128, 129.
Warenne, Earl (in 1300), 151–2.
—, — (1335), 103 ff.
—, —, 31.
—, —, his retainder, 138.
Warkworth Castle, 138.
Warnford, co. Hants, 34.
Warrington, tournament at, 148.

INDEX

Warwick, Guy Earl of (d. 1315), 149.
—, Earl of, 137, 139.
Watlington, manor of, co. Oxon., 122.
Westminster Abbey, corrodar at, 38.
Whitchurch, co. Oxon., Aumale manor of, 125, 126.
Wigod, 122.
Wigton, John of, 152.
Willoughby, Philip de, 38.
—, Robert de, 152.
Winchelsey, Abp., Robert, 173.
Windsor, poor knights of, 147.
—, tournaments at, 85, 120, 144–5.
Wither, Sir William, 20.
Wolf, John, feodary (1380), 127.

Woodstock, tournament at, 148.
Worcester Abbey, 38, 130 n. 4.
Wriothesley, Sir Thomas, Garter (d. 1534), 152.
Wykes, Thomas de, 39.
Wyvile, Mr. Robert de, 38.

Yarnton, co. Oxon., 123.
York, government at (1332–8), as in 1297–1304, 96 and n. 2.
— statute of (1322), 61, 81, 82.

Zouche, Lord la, professional brawler, 80.
—, Alan la, 152.

PRINTED IN GREAT BRITAIN
AT THE UNIVERSITY PRESS, OXFORD
BY VIVIAN RIDLER
PRINTER TO THE UNIVERSITY

Soc
HT
657
D45